Performance

Performance

Ruth Ivo

CORONET

First published in Great Britain in 2024 by Coronet
An imprint of Hodder & Stoughton
An Hachette UK company

1

Copyright © Ruth Ivo 2024

A CIP catalogue record for this title is available from the British Library

Hardback ISBN 9781399720700
ebook ISBN 9781399720724

Typeset in Sabon MT by Hewer Text UK Ltd, Edinburgh
Printed and bound in Great Britain by Clays Ltd, Elcograf S.p.A.

Hodder & Stoughton policy is to use papers that are natural, renewable
and recyclable products and made from wood grown in sustainable
forests. The logging and manufacturing processes are expected to
conform to the environmental regulations of the country of origin.

Hodder & Stoughton Ltd
Carmelite House
50 Victoria Embankment
London EC4Y 0DZ

www.hodder.co.uk

For MTB 219 and all who sailed in her

Beginners

My name wasn't always Ruby. It is no longer as I write this now. I have a habit of shedding them like skin. *Ruby*. Valentine roses, magic slippers. Bass-note of blood. There's meaning in a name, so choose wisely. It might have a different plan for you. Before I found Ruby, I'd always felt my birth name ill-fitting, reluctant to recognise myself in its adult-sounding arrangement of consonants and vowels. As a child I played at different possibilities with those who didn't know me, each name a character with a story of its own, and a line drawn against the past. Later, I learned there are risks to choices based on narrative potential. You forget your character does not always have your best interests at heart. In the end Ruby had to die, but for a while she was my story. And this is hers.

Imagine for a moment a theatre, small, worn, its velvet seats slightly soiled. A gilt proscenium arch frames a stage with well-loved curtains, royal boxes either side, a mirrored bar at the far end of the auditorium. In this establishment you are trusted with glass but there's a crunch underfoot, a boozy hue to the audience. Patrolling the aisles, aggressive ushers armed with cattle prods give warning looks to those still on their smartphones.

There's a rippling of red curtain as we move, now, to the wings where a girl is awaiting her entrance.

See her alone in darkness, dressed for battle, her grease-paint thick, eyes fixed on the man sitting at a table centre stage. She's preparing, ready to slip into the persona of whoever he needs her to be.

The man at the table taps his fingers, checks the time on his watch. The girl scrutinises these gestures, trying to learn what she can in the moments before. He looks up sharply and their eyes meet. I'd like to freeze time and step into the scene and fold her in my arms, but we must withdraw and leave her to the story.

In the gloom it's hard to make out the set. Shadowy figures motionless as mannequins are poised, ready to animate. Out front, there's a wave of anticipatory coughing as the lights go down. No. Let's make this audience rowdy, more bear pit than Broadway. Heckling and whistles, some of them are even smoking.

The curtains begin to whirr and then part. Lights up on the man at the table. The girl in the wings takes a breath. Showtime.

Act 1

Chapter 1

To observe someone at breakfast is an intimate thing, especially if they don't know you're there. The second time I saw Gabriel Grosse he was eating a plate of eggs, a napkin tucked into his collar like a little boy.

I studied him from the doorway, trying to gain some small advantage. *He* seemed lonely in the jabbering midday crowd, their voices amplified with the confidence of daytime drinking at one of London's elite members' clubs. 'He's in the dining room,' the receptionist said when I told her who I was meeting, her gaze decoding my outfit, age and attractiveness on a scale of one-to-ten. Mistress? Unlikely. Also, it was not mistress-o'clock. Then who? That morning I'd dressed carefully in a black cashmere sweater and fox-fur stole. Orange lipstick. My take on an interview outfit.

He looked up and saw me staring and I waved – *Cooee* – as if we were old friends.

'I'm sorry, so rude of me,' he said, mopping his chin and attempting to stand.

I sat down in front of him. 'Don't worry,' I conveyed in my most soothing tone that I wasn't offended by eggs.

We took each other in over the remains of his breakfast. Amused brown eyes in an average face. No flicker of recognition or scent of evil. Just a man in a suit that said *money*.

'Do you have a cat?' His voice a transatlantic drawl.

I looked down and saw the fox-fur stole had shed liberally over my sweater.

'It's vintage,' I said and saw him smirk at my discomfort.

'So, Ruby, you direct *burlesque*?' he said as if the word made him slightly ill.

'No,' I shook my head. 'I do weird stuff.'

'Oh *good*.'

I'd prepared a slideshow on my laptop that I placed on the crumb-strewn table, hoping he wouldn't notice the crack in the screen. I launched into my explanation of the first image as it appeared, a Pierrot holding a bunch of balloons suspended high above a crowd.

'Uh huh.' His tone suggested there was nothing I could show him he had not already seen. I tried again. A ship on fire, pole-dancing mermaid for a figurehead, a trapeze artist in a cage like human ribs. Daydreams painstakingly teased into reality.

'Uh huh.' A note of impatience this time. I shortened my descriptions, and we flicked through at speed.

'Oh, that's sexy,' he exclaimed at two ghostly painted figures dancing in a snowstorm at night. I told him the origins of the piece. He didn't care. We went back to the pictures.

'That's sexy,' he said again.

'It's from a music video.'

'That's kind of what we do at the Club. Each number is like a music video.'

'Yes, I see that.'

'You've been?'

'Of course.'

He looked at me slyly. 'You know you have a twitch?'

I nodded. 'I've always had it.' In times of stress my own eyelids flickered like a doll's.

'I used to have one too.'

'You still do . . . a little,' I said, and saw him smile.

I could count the number of job interviews I'd had on one hand, but this was no longer just that. He was pushing buttons, trying to figure me out according to his criteria. Fuckability. Class. I already knew *his* reputation: he was a Rich Man, a Bad Man, but what else?

He started telling me about the show at the Club, growing animated. He mentioned the words 'Art' and 'Feminism' while I gave my best impression of someone who liked him. It's possible I did.

We parted company on the pavement outside the Groucho. After an hour in its nocturnal gloom, I was surprised to find it still light.

'So, I'll see you Wednesday,' he said, opening a packet of Marlboro Reds, slipping one between his lips. We were awkward now standing in the street, more comfortable in the shadows.

'Look forward to it.' I held out my hand to him.

Something passed across his face, and I wondered if he were unused to shaking hands with women. He walked away, a slick charcoal figure in the Soho afternoon, the memory of his fingers, cold and perfectly smooth, lingering on my own. Not what I'd expected, but perhaps the feeling was mutual.

I wandered down Old Compton Street through the stream of human traffic, stepping round tourists come to witness the dying days of the former red-light district. Wardour and Dean Street, Frith Street and Greek, the square mile named for a Tudor hunting cry, where legends of a certain kind were born. *Soho*. Shorthand for sleaze for more than a century, now undergoing a process of erasure, sex shops and strip clubs vanishing overnight; coffee franchises and boutiques selling minimalist trainers appearing in their place as if they'd never been. But there were still traces of its old raffish charm to give me the thrill it always had. Oh Soho! The grubby heart of this beautiful beast of a city.

I stopped at Bar Italia where I purchased an overpriced panini and ate it on my way to Shaftesbury Avenue. From there, I caught a bus to Chelsea, the red double-decker crawling through West End traffic past theatres and billboards, on to Piccadilly, Hyde Park, Knightsbridge, Sloane Square. The grand shops getting smaller as we moved further along the King's Road. The bus turned left down Beaufort Street and I got off at Battersea Bridge next to the river. Brown and murky concealing dangerous currents, it was lovely that day, shining silver in the spring sun.

Down Cheyne Walk and the famous Chelsea Embankment built over London's first great sewer, elegant mansions to one side, a row of ramshackle candy-coloured houseboats on the other, to the entrance of the moorings. Through the wooden gates, I quickened my step as I passed the boatyard manager's office. She'd taken to ambushing me in recent weeks, chasing last month's mooring fees. Over the small metal footbridges across the pontoons to where the old military boat sat at a drunken tilt in the brown river mud. Approaching the gangplank, I felt a twinge of guilt at the sight of her scruffy hull and ragged washing line where one weather-bleached tea towel flapped in the breeze. Close up, you could see the paint peeling on the pink front door and the rotting wood around the portholes, but there was still nowhere I'd rather live.

In the corner of the living room Kristian was hunched over his wig, using a tiny hook to lace each individual hair into a lace cap on a mannequin head. Next to him was a life-sized flamingo, liberated from the Royal Opera House by a former crewmate. A greying chaise longue and rusted birdcage added to the room's junk-shop air.

'I think I might have got it,' I said, pausing in the doorway for effect.

Kristian looked up, his gentle eyes wild. 'Gosh,' he said. 'Did he remember you?'

'Nope.' I flopped onto the chaise. 'He was almost nice. It was weird.'

'Hello, bunny!' came a bright voice from below.

Felicity appeared at the top of the stairs with a jug full of ice cubes and foliage, her curves spilling from a pair of denim hot pants and tight gingham shirt.

'Special gin,' she announced. 'With herbs and things. Now tell me everything.'

I accepted my cocktail in an almost-clean jam jar and proceeded with my blow-by-blow account of the day's encounter. Functioning as both family and audience to each other's lives, the boat crew and I lived for such exploits, our anecdotes displayed like medals.

'Hilarious that he didn't recognise you,' Felicity said, replenishing our glasses.

'I wasn't wearing clothes the last time.'

'Hmm. It doesn't seem *entirely* safe.'

'But isn't it important there are still places that aren't?'

There was a new 'safe' London of recent years; its underground venues were being shut down, victim to licensing laws that were enforced only where the land was worth more than gold. The new nightlife would be conducted during designated hours at a reasonable decibel level, far away from the sanctity of the residential street. Nowhere, it seemed, was safe from the sweeping eye of local government. Yes, London nightlife was under siege, those who loved it powerless against its decline. And oh, how I'd loved it, those Otherworlds that appeared after dark, the fever of the dance floor, sex emerging from the shadows to exist on the surface of things; how people changed, becoming more themselves, or someone else entirely. Where you could meet your own secret desires – *who is it that you really are?* – and articulate without words all the joys and sorrows of the daylight world.

One year earlier, amidst the siege, the extraordinary news had arrived that Gabriel Grosse's club – titan of the New York party scene – would be bringing a sister venue to Soho. It seemed improbable that somewhere so famously debauched could open its doors in the heart of the West End, but open it did, quickly achieving an almost mythological allure due to the secrecy of what went on inside. With no photography permitted, everything known about it was born of rumour: hair-raising tales of identical twin sisters committing incest live on stage while the very rich and very famous ran riot through its lawless corridors. '*The new Studio 54!*' the press had screamed as if to be 'the new' anything was a high form of praise. People grew shameless when they spoke of it, overkeen to let you know they'd been. The casting call came to every performer in London: acrobats, dancers, freak-show and fire acts. Someone at the Club was doing their research and casting the net wide.

I'd arrived at the designated hour at an anonymous stage door around the corner from the Club's main entrance. Hovering outside was a pissed-off girl holding a basket. 'Are you here for the audition?' I asked her.

'This is my third call-back. I've been waiting ten minutes for someone to let me in.'

There was a buzzing sound and the door clicked open.

The girl with the basket knew where she was going, so I followed her up a sticky flight of stairs to a dingy corridor, stale with the unpleasant smell typical of night-time venues outside trading hours. More stairs, more corridor – the place was a labyrinth – and, finally, a narrow dressing room papered with layers of mismatched vintage wallpaper, crowded with performers of every kind. A make-up mirror framed with bulbs covered the length of one wall. At the far end, an enormous white rabbit was calmly powdering his face.

The girl placed the basket on the shelf in front of the mirror, opened it, and took out a large yellow snake that she cradled like a baby.

'Do you know what they're looking for?' I said as I changed into my costume.

'I don't think they know.'

When it was my turn, I was directed to the landing where a short flight of steps led directly to the back of a darkened stage. I walked forward squinting into the spotlight, unable to make out the faces of those sat in the front row.

'What's your name, honey?' a thin voice asked.

'Ruby.'

'Ruby. You do fire?'

'No. I'm a singer.'

'Another fucking singer?' another voice exploded. 'She's not even *Black*.'

There was the click of a lighter, the flare briefly illuminating the face of a man, his expression ugly with anger.

'You do anything else?' the first voice said.

'Burlesque.'

'Burlesque?' the angry man again. 'I *told* you idiots . . .' He launched into a tirade on the theme of general incompetence.

I remained listening to him rant until it became clear they'd forgotten me, so went back to the dressing room and changed into my street clothes.

'Good luck,' I told the remaining auditions before I left.

Later, I made enquiries on the performer grapevine. Oh, *that* was Gabriel Grosse, self-styled impresario. A special breed of arsehole.

The week the Club opened, I'd gone back, fully intending to despise what I saw. I wore a black lace catsuit with metal spikes on the nipples and crotch, with towering boots, a mixture of kink and *stay the fuck away*. My memory of the night a Bacchanalian blur. There'd been a four-poster bed – I'd been on it at some point – and an impression of fire everywhere. A red glow over the fevered faces in the VIP, a minor rock star sliding his hand up my thigh at the bar. I bumped into some showgirls I knew, giddy at being on the *inside* of something special. But it was the show that dazzled me.

Down in the main space, a cauldron of bodies and sound, craning my neck to see what was happening on stage: bare breasts under strobes. The feeling that anything might happen. And then a shaft of pale light in the middle of the crowd, and a lingering image of a man and waif-like girl making love in the air, like something Holy.

I'd wanted it then, a feeling close to possession.

For is it not a most human quality to want that which rejects us?

Then the email arrived, and the whole world tilted as if the words themselves exerted a gravitational pull.

Gabriel Grosse is looking for a director for his show. Shall I give him your contact?

Who would say no to choices such as these, for in fact they were not choices at all.

Chapter 2

To work at night is to live back to front. When most people are returning home to their cosy sofas and dinner in front of a screen, that's when the late-night entertainers, the bar staff and sex workers, graveyard shift drivers, go-go dancers and dealers are heading out into the wild hours to service the world on the other side of the looking glass.

On the river, the little boat tethered to land by a thread rides the high tide, as the sun sets behind Battersea Power Station like the dimming of the houselights – a signal that something is about to happen. Onboard, preparations are under way for the long night ahead. Kristian is in the kitchen, where only the moulded metal ceiling hints of the boat's former military glory. Along a narrow corridor past the open door to Felicity's cabin, she reclines in a silken robe on the bed, fingers tap-tapping at her phone. Onwards past the shabby bathroom to the cabin at the far end, where in a cracked and speckled mirror, a performer is applying the familiar paint to turn her features into a cartoon approximation of sex appeal.

I dragged my wheelie suitcase from beneath the bed, wincing at the whiff of stale Prosecco from inside. My showgirl outfit was still in there, bunched up from the last time I performed, along with my threadbare feather fans and emergency gaffer-tape.

'Kitty wake up,' I poked the Cat's sleeping form. 'I need you to help me with the egg.' He'd snuck into my cabin through the skylight, oil-stained denim jacket under the sheets, a croissant for a present. 'Get the fuck off my boat,' were usually how his visits ended, having driven me to distraction once again. He'd disappear for a week or two, then show up bearing food and some other strange gift by way of apology – his equivalent of leaving a dead mouse on the doorstep. When he wasn't on board, the Cat lived in a battered delivery van that he used for his nefarious activities.

In the dark, the fibreglass egg – roughly the size of an armchair – appeared to glow. Too large to fit through the front door, it lived on deck, as familiar a sight as the broken-down barbecue and fraying deckchairs. Lately, its iridescent paint had begun to flake, its velvet lining long gone, but it still looked passable under the stage lights. I'd never taken care of my props and costumes, cabaret only ever a stepping stone to somewhere else. I hadn't imagined I'd be pushing thirty and still performing to pay the bills. Oh, but it was fun! Hired to go to parties, to dance on tables and swing from chandeliers. Hundreds of pounds for the length of a song and the freedom to do whatever you wanted on stage; no formal training necessary. The only rule: that it must entertain.

Now the Cat hoisted the egg onto his shoulder and steadying it with both hands, carried it slowly down the gangplank. I knocked on the window and waved goodbye to the rest of the crew, then followed with the egg's filigree metal stand, tugging my suitcase behind.

The van was parked in the loading bay next to the entrance of the moorings, which the Cat used as his private parking space to the vexation of the boatyard management. He lowered the electronic ramp to lift the egg into the back, and I clambered into the cab, pushing the rubbish littering the seats to the floor. I checked the time on my phone. An hour till I was due onstage.

The venue was tucked underneath the Westway flyover at the scruffier end of the Portobello Road, though it described its location as 'Notting Hill'. It had been decorated by someone with an uncompromising aesthetic vision and was decked out wall to wall in white, the audience lounging on large white beds to watch shows performed in the round on the slippery white floor. I'd known it in several incarnations since its early days as a rave venue, but the fortunes of nightclubs can turn on a dime, and this latest version had been conceived to attract the type of clientele who preferred their thrills served up to them in a laboratory environment.

Maciek, resident of the boat's smallest cabin was in the dressing room, drinking Pimm's laced with gin as he'd been on the night we first met. The venue was new then, Maciek not long arrived from Warsaw, a Polish baby-Warhol slaving as an intern, lumbered with the task of stage-managing the show. The booker at the time liked declaring to anyone who'd listen that the venue would 'change the face of this dump', by which he meant the neighbourhood. Two years later he was long gone with Maciek promoted to his job. The neighbourhood itself remained the same.

'Hello, cabin boy,' I smiled.

'Timing,' Maciek said.

'I'm on in twenty, right?' I dumped my bag by an empty seat at the mirror. 'I've already done my make-up.'

'Where's the egg?'

'The Cat's got it. He's waiting by the fire exit.'

16

'Mmm. Obedient.'

I blew him a kiss and started to wriggle out of my clothes.

'How are ya, Ruby?' said Stah, a shaven-headed aerialist from Australia, who was wearing nothing but head-to-toe gold glitter.

'Oh, you know,' I said, tugging down my jeans. 'Still here.'

The dressing room could have been one of a thousand I'd seen, performers spending much of their time in nowhere spaces such as these, preparing for the brief moments when they'd burst onto stage like human fireworks. Small and cramped with an unwholesome smell. A wall of lockers for the kitchen and bar staff. Violent strip lighting. Still, it wasn't a toilet, so that was something.

Sitting at the mirror next to Stah, Johanna was putting the finishing touches to her face, hands down one of the most beautiful women I'd seen. The venue's resident hostess, she'd once shown me her vagina after cocktails in the dressing room one night, whipping off her knickers to display the softly folded opening between her legs.

'It's perfect,' I'd said, impressed.

'Made in Thailand,' Johanna smiled, displaying her lovely teeth.

Some showgirls I knew spent hours setting elaborate vintage hairstyles and powdering their skin until it shimmered, but, having neither the patience nor the skills, I pinned a feathered cap over my hair, before slapping on feathered nipple-covers with another layer of tape. No corset or stockings, just a pair of satin shorts with a ragged feather train over bare legs. Always contrary, I enjoyed arriving nearly naked in front of an audience; without a costume to tease out of, you had to find other ways of earning their applause.

17

Stah was bending over to insert a deflated gold balloon into an orifice, and I averted my eyes to the mirror to give her some privacy.

When it was my turn, Maciek came to fetch me and I followed him down the backstairs, past the kitchen to outside the double doors that led to the stage where the egg was waiting for me, secured to its stand with cable ties. I handed him my music on a memory stick and he disappeared to give it to the DJ.

Listening to the babble of the audience on the other side of the doors, I kept my back against the wall to allow the waiters to pass. The staff who'd been there a while no longer blinked at the sight of a semi-clad showgirl, but occasionally there'd be a trainee who didn't know where to look.

'Will you save me some of those?' I asked a newbie as he shuffled by carrying a tray of pan-Asian finger food.

'You can have one now if you like,' he said, ears turning red.

'Ruby?' Maciek came swinging back through, in the company of a bouncer he'd commandeered to help.

I swallowed what I'd been eating, sucked my fingers and clambered into the egg through the small door in its side. Folding my limbs into the cramped space, I felt it shift slightly to the right. Maciek closed the door and gave the shell a friendly rap. I winced, raising my middle finger towards the sound.

I braced myself as the egg was wobbled into place in the centre of the room, where it sat gradually heating up beneath the lights. Hunched inside, I breathed in its particular smell of fibreglass and mildew, mixed with my own sweat and melting make-up. My feather fans were folded in front of me, their fluffy edges tickling my nostrils. All sound from outside was amplified within the shell, and I could hear the laughter and comments from the audience at the sight of the tipsy egg in the middle of the floor.

How long I'd be trapped varied wildly. There'd been times when I'd been left for up to twenty minutes, growing dizzy and cramped waiting for my musical cue. My heart was beating hard as it always did before a performance. I concentrated on slowing my breath and sent up a little prayer to whoever's job it was to watch over the dancing monkeys of the world.

It was often inside the egg I'd find myself questioning my life choices, a critical voice that made unhelpful comments on the theme of wasted potential and the value of dignity. But no matter how blasé I'd become it was hard to maintain ambivalence faced with the reality of a live audience; on that knife's edge between humiliation and glory.

Outside the egg, I sensed the houselights growing dim, the crack around the door glowing white from the follow-spot's beam, and it struck me that if the job at the Club worked out, this might be the last time I'd have to perform.

Taking a deep breath, I put one hand on the door, and pushed.

*

There is a transformation that happens on stage, when all else falls away.

The reveal is a gradual one, extending first a leg and then a hand, fingernails scratching their way across the shell.

Your fans conceal your face and body, until the moment the music soars and you open them to fly.

To dance like no one is watching is one thing, but to dance when everyone is, quite another.

You stretch and expand inside your skin, pushing your ribs to the sky. Your body is the shape of an S, every curve dipped, but this is not about sex. You are the reflected fragments of every story you were ever told, of creatures half-woman half-bird; blood-red shells and faces launching ships across the world. It is the story you tell yourself, of the significance of your nightly rebirth, part of a wider story – a mythology of self – without which all is chaos. It is the story you are telling them.

After all, who would not want to see a real girl hatch?

The microphone waits on its stand. You move towards it. This is the time to look the audience in the face. You can dance lost in your own world but pity the singer who cannot meet a gaze.

Now, power is hitting your system like a drug.

With one finger, you stroke the side of the microphone checking it's turned on, then, visualising the first note in your mind, you open your mouth to sing.

'*Birds flying high you know how I feel . . .*'

*

Maciek and I fizzed all the way home, squealing at each red light the Cat roared through, stopping only when there were no other cars around. The van screeched to a halt next to the moorings and we tumbled from the cab, Maciek carrying my bag as we weaved our way across the footbridges, the Cat following behind with the egg.

Back on board, Maciek announced he was going for a jog, disappearing into the night in running shoes and *Comme des Garcons*, while the Cat and I dragged rugs and various blankets onto deck for a nightcap. By night, the river panorama was a miracle of lights, the fairy-tale cascades of Albert Bridge glowing in the distance, red eyes winking from the many cranes beyond. Huddled in a quilt, I looked out over the curving sweep of glimmering water, the sky just starting to shift towards dawn.

Seven years since my first night on board, so happy that I'd wept. Seven years of watching the seasons change over the Thames, mornings greeted from the wrong side, red wine staining our lips, bleary eyes blinking in wonder at the orange clouds. When had all this become ordinary? There were still times, clear nights like this with the burn of whisky in my throat and the warm body asleep beside me, I could almost recall I lived on an island of dreams. But as my high began to fade and tomorrow's hangover crept forward like the brown river tide, it seemed only like I'd been there too long.

Chapter 3

Late one morning I was half asleep in bed, lulled by the hollow sound of water hitting metal, the thump and suck of Thames against hull. Stretching out my legs, I recoiled from the damp patch at my feet beneath the rotting skylight. Through the glass, the grey London sky tilted back and forth.

I pushed my head beneath the pillow then threw it off again, memory bludgeoning me awake. Kicking the covers away, I snatched my kimono from the hook on the door, almost colliding with Maciek as he emerged from his cabin, eyes hidden behind round John Lennon sunglasses.

'Morning, captain,' he said, voice thick with sleep.

'It's today, it's today, it's today . . .' I muttered on my way to the kitchen where I switched on the kettle, fidgeting at the counter while I waited for it to boil.

Maciek drifted in and opened the fridge, removing a selection of vegetables.

'Potato?' I enquired when he began feeding them into the juicer.

'Mmm.'

'I'm not sure raw is a good idea.'

He produced a strip of foil-packaged pills and added two.

'What's that?'

'Codeine.'

'Have you got codeine?' The Cat appeared in the doorway; a towel wrapped round his waist.

'Don't give him codeine,' I said.

Maciek pressed the button on the juicer, drowning the
kitchen in noise.

Escaping upstairs with my tea, I found Kristian already
hard at work. The boat's longest-standing crewmate, we'd
met ten years before in a Kentish Town squat, a five-storey
building that had once accommodated student nurses. Each
floor had a different character, loosely defined by the
nationality of its residents and their preferred recreational
activities. There was the 'Spanish' floor that blasted Techno
and reeked of skunk; the sunny, well-kept 'Antipodean'
floor where Kristian lived; the self-explanatory 'heroin'
floor; and the top floor housing an all-female coterie of
costumiers and showgirls. It was a strangely innocent time,
all of us halfway between childhood and whatever came
next. We wandered round in fancy dress, painted on the
walls, and went partying to gigs in Camden, electro nights
in Soho and psychedelic raves with UV chill-out rooms. It
all came to an ignoble end as many squats do, with in-fight-
ing, a fire on the Spanish floor and, finally, the bailiffs when
the developers moved in.

'How's the wig?' I said, taking a seat on the chaise.

Kristian emitted a high-pitched giggle.

'Have you had breakfast?' I asked.

'Coffee.'

'I'll make us something,' I said. 'Soon as Maciek's
finished liquidising his vegetables.'

It is the curse of the creative brain that left unoccupied it
will start to eat itself. As a working actor Kristian was often
away, but always returned to the boat, using the time

23

between auditions with plans for his self-penned musical. Recently, he'd decided a wig for the leading role was the next logical step and was painstakingly building one from scratch, a sign he'd retreated to the state of high-functioning procrastination that was the flipside of his meticulous nature. I blamed the last hard winter for taking its toll on the crew, amplifying pre-existing quirks. There were only so many nights of the wind biting through the wooden hull to freeze you in your bed, shuffling around in coats and hats, conducting much of our lives in close proximity to the boat's two ancient electric heaters, before something had to give. For this and other reasons, boat life was not for everyone; with every cough, sneeze and sigh audible through the plywood cabin walls, we were intimate with each other's sleep patterns, dental hygiene, and sex lives. Usually, the arrival of spring brought with it amnesia, we'd open the French doors and take our tea onto the deck and in the peace of the morning the memory of the cold would melt away as surely as the frost. But this year our torpor had lingered, everyone was broke and even the boat felt ill. Maciek had grown increasingly abstract, wandering the corridors, muttering nihilistic barbs, swathed in layers of weird couture. I'd lie in bed beneath the champagne bucket that was no longer catching the drips. Was this still fun? I wasn't sure. I worried for our collective mental health.

In the watery light of my cabin, I rummaged through the mould-ravaged silk and tulle of my overflowing clothes rail, tossing the rejected items on the growing pile on my bed, eventually settling on the closest thing I had to neutral black. I returned to the kitchen where Kristian and the Cat were eyeing each other warily over a plate of bacon sandwiches.

'Do I look smart?' I said.

Kristian looked me over with a critical eye. 'I can see your bra.'

'Should I wear something underneath?'

'I think probably.'

'How about the rest?'

'The rest is good.'

I left the moorings, crossing the busy main road to the shortcut between the red-brick towers of the World's End estate that gave its name to the area. Once the site of a notorious eighteenth-century pleasure garden, later part of sixties bohemia of which the houseboats were all that remained. I'd always loved the name with its apocalyptic overtones, imagining the city submerged, the boat sailing off into the mist.

Sitting on the top deck of the bus as it moved towards the centre of the city, I had the feeling I was about to do something irreversible. I recognised the high-wire sensation – I'd had it seven years before when I'd first walked on board the boat. The knowledge of your life about to change, like a sudden awareness of the Earth shifting beneath you.

From Piccadilly, I cut into Soho through a riot of building works where shiny new frontages were emerging. The stage door was on a different street from the Club's main entrance in a desolate alley; one of the few places in the former red-light district where you could still purchase an available body, speedball and a sandwich on the same short stretch of pavement.

Gazing into the security camera, I pressed the buzzer. 'Hello?' an aggressive female voice came over the intercom.

'I'm here to see Gabriel Grosse.'

There was a click as the door unlocked, opening onto a grimy stairwell with steps that sucked at my feet. At the top was a corridor with several dirty white doors, at the far end, a flight of narrow stairs and faint murmuring coming from above. I began to climb, heading for the voices at the top of the building.

On the third floor, in a run-down office with regulation grey carpet, half-a-dozen people were sitting at computers. I noted more than one of them was on Facebook.

A phone rang and a blonde girl snatched it from its cradle. 'Hello, the Club,' she demanded in a King's Road drawl. 'Mmm hmm. No, I'm afraid that's simply *not* possible.' She smashed the phone down and it immediately rang again. 'Hello, the Club. *Delling!*' her voice switched to delight.

'Excuse me?' I said.

Several pairs of eyes swung in my direction.

'I'm here to see Gabriel Grosse?'

The blonde girl put her hand over the receiver. 'Are you an audition?'

'No.'

'Call you back.' She put the phone back in its cradle and said, 'What's it about?'

'I'm here for a trial. For the director job.'

I saw some of them exchange a glance that I did not understand.

The blonde girl led me back down the stairs, turning at the bottom onto a passageway that was painted black. She indicated a doorway at the end and left without a word. I stepped through and found myself next to the stage.

Gabriel Grosse was on a sofa in the middle of the room. 'Oh hey, we're just starting,' he said when he saw me.

Crossing the floor to where he sat, my eyes roamed the space, unfamiliar under the houselights. A large room with a domed ceiling and an amphitheatre feel, decorated to resemble a decaying theatre in shades of dirty gold. Tiered booths on either side led to the deep stage in front of which several mismatched sofas clustered around low tables – the expensive seats. The top of the walls was edged with rows of bulbs, with a large follow-spot mounted at one end of the room. It was very cold with the smell of stale booze, cigarette smoke and bleach masking something nastier. On stage, an athletic boy and girl were waiting beneath a proscenium arch, wearing their best audition smiles.

Gabriel Grosse gestured for me to sit next to him. I joined him on the sofa and my eyes were drawn to the table in front of us that was collaged with vintage porn. 'Okay, let's see what you've got,' he said to the pair who obediently took their places. 'Let's go,' he called to someone at the back of the room.

Music piped over the speakers as the duo launched into a polished acro-balance routine.

'Pretty mediocre,' Gabriel Grosse murmured in my ear. 'Don't you think?'

On stage the male acrobat was swinging the female in a circle by an arm and a foot, her body locked in a dancer's pose.

'You don't like it?' I avoided the question.

'I'm fucking bored. The only way I'd book *that* is if the girl got her tits out.'

She was on the male acrobat's shoulder now, perched elegantly on one quivering leg.

'*You* go and explain,' he said as the routine came to an end. 'Otherwise, they can stop wasting my fucking time.'

The acrobats were waiting, breathing heavily, their faces flushed and eager. I got to my feet. It was ten paces to where they stood.

'Hey, come back for Christ's sake.'

I turned around. He was laughing.

'Not fair to do that to you on your first day.'

I grimaced, relief colliding with a perverse sense of gratitude.

'Yeah, we'll call you,' Gabriel Grosse said, searching in his pockets.

'Did you want us to come back?' said the male acrobat, seemingly unaware of the universal language of rejection.

'If you get some fucking talent,' Gabriel Grosse muttered around the cigarette now between his lips.

'What did you say?' The acrobat's muscles seemed to swell and the girl placed a hand on her partner's arm.

She led him from the stage glancing back as she did, and I felt myself shrink. I'm not one of them, I telegraphed with my eyes.

Gabriel Grosse was fumbling with his lighter. 'This fucking town,' he said. 'This fucking town.'

He led me back to the corridor with the white doors, barging through one of them into some kind of prop cupboard, where a boy and girl were lounging on office chairs inside.

'Guys, this is our trainee director,' he announced to their startled faces.

I gave them an awkward wave. 'Ruby.'

There was a beat then they seemed to click into gear.

'Hi!' the girl said. She had wide brown eyes and tiny white teeth like a child's.

'This is Lila,' Gabriel Grosse said. 'And our stage manager, Archie. You'll show her the ropes, won't you?'

They nodded. Oh, absolutely, sir.

'They'll tell you all about me,' he winked, and they laughed on cue.

'So, what's next?' he said.

The stage manager, who had the face of a choirboy, glanced at a whiteboard pinned to the wall on which a curious collection of words was scrawled. *Dog*, *Spirit Gum*, *LubeLubeLUBE* and *Barbie*. 'We've got Barbie for a workshop in the VIP.'

Gabriel Grosse looked at me. 'Well, let's go see her.'

We went back to the main room and through a set of doors leading to a grand staircase. The vomit smell was worse here, and I suppressed the urge to gag as we continued to the floor above.

The VIP was small, with a tiny bar and handful of tables, decorated in the same decaying grandeur style. A second room led off to one side dominated by a four-poster bed. At the far end, green velvet curtains bordered a small stage on which stood a large pink box with a clear window on the front. Inside, a living doll was coming to life to the helium-strains of 'Barbie Girl' by Aqua.

Taking tiny steps, the doll tiptoed from the box, an oversize pink hairbrush in one hand. She was blonde and pretty, with the lines of a classically trained dancer. The number ended with a strip down to a flesh-coloured thong and nipple-pasties.

'How would you make it cool?' said Gabriel Grosse.

I looked at Barbie who smiled winsomely.

'When I was little, I used to melt my Barbies,' I said thinking out loud. 'And cut their hair and turn them into punks.'

'Uh huh.'

29

'Also, Barbies have no genitals,' I continued. 'She could have a Barbie sex toy but can't make it work because there's nothing between her legs except moulded plastic.'

'Okay. How does it end?'

I thought quickly, grasping for the darkest thing I could find. 'She decides life isn't worth living and blows her brains out. All over the inside of the box.'

'All right,' he said. 'She's all yours. You've got an hour.'

It wasn't much time, but it was enough to re-block the number to incorporate the new ending. While we worked, Gabriel Grosse sat at the back of the room, his face lit from beneath by his phone.

'Kinda goofy,' he said when we'd finished. 'But it's cute. We'll put it in tonight.' He turned to Barbie. 'You're free, aren't you?'

'Oh, yes!' said Barbie. 'I mean, I *can* be. But what about the new costume and props?'

'Oh, we've got that covered right?'

'No problem,' I lied.

'I'll be back at seven,' he said to me.

'What's happening at seven?'

'Come for dinner,' he said, and left.

Barbie and I looked at each other. 'Don't worry,' I told her anxious, grateful face.

'Oh, for fucksake,' said Archie when I told him about the new number going in. 'There's no time.'

'We're going to need a gun.'

'We've got a gun. Obviously.'

'The prosthetics are a problem . . .'

'Costume department,' he said. 'Second floor.'

30

The second floor was another white corridor, cluttered with a washing machine, ironing board and a number of large items including a fibre-glass mushroom, a tarnished golden throne and rancid-looking toilet.

I knocked on the door I'd been directed to. 'Come in,' a cheerful voice called from inside.

I pushed open the door and stepped into a mess of sequins and fringe, polystyrene heads wearing elaborate feather headdresses scattered about the room. Standing in the middle of it all, a tall man with an extravagant silver quiff was pinning a beaded showgirl outfit onto a mannequin.

'Hello,' I said. 'Archie said to speak to you about a new number going in tonight.'

'Hello! Yes! Okay . . .'

'It's a Barbie number. We need to make her look naked – Barbie-naked – no genitals or nipples. I was thinking some kind of prosthetic?'

His face became panicked. 'Uh . . . I might have a flesh-coloured thong somewhere?'

I went back downstairs to Archie. 'He doesn't do prosthetics,' I said.

'No, he makes costumes.' He was beginning to irritate me.

'Is there any petty cash?' I said. 'There might be something on Berwick Street.'

'Just keep the receipts,' he enunciated in clipped RP.

I left by the main entrance, down a sweeping staircase lit with dim orange light from a line of crystal chandeliers. At the bottom, a golden anti-aircraft gun dominated the foyer. A hazy memory of a waistcoated pig sitting astride it rose like a bubble from somewhere in my subconscious. At the fancy dress shop on Berwick Street, I purchased a pair of oversized foam breasts from the tiny woman behind the counter.

When I returned, Archie seemed in a better mood and had assembled most items on the list.

'We still need something for the final reveal,' I said, looking anxiously at the clock.

'I'll figure something out.'

'Thank you,' I said, and meant it.

Outside on Old Compton Street the bars were spilling onto the pavement, the air sticky with the sour smell of beer. Gabriel Grosse had come to fetch me not long after seven, accompanied by the girl called Lila. I tried to get a grasp on their relationship, were they lovers? Something told me no, though they shared an easy-going rapport that was almost familial.

When I asked, Lila told me she'd been dancing at the Club for eight years.

'Lila's old guard,' Gabriel Grosse said. We'd stopped at the crossroads where Soho became Covent Garden. 'You girls wanna go to The Ivy?'

'Sure,' I said, as if Wednesday night work dinners at The Ivy were the most natural thing in the world.

'I just love their steaks,' said Lila.

The maître d' seemed to open like a flower as we passed through the doors of the famous stained-glass frontage. Her eyes fluttered to the reservations book. 'Welcome back, sir,' she said.

We followed her through to the crowded dining area, where a table was produced from nowhere. I cast my eyes around the elegant room, its velvet seats and low-hanging glass lamps, then back at the menu wondering what I could get away with ordering.

'Christ, the menu is so fucking tired. They haven't changed it in years.'

I glanced at Gabriel Grosse, then at Lila, whose expression gave nothing away.

'I don't wanna eat this crap.' He tossed the menu on the table and shoved his chair backwards into a passing waiter. For a moment Lila and I held each other's gaze, then hurried after him.

Outside, Gabriel Grosse tore open a fresh packet of cigarettes with shaking hands. 'Fuck,' he swore, wrestling with his lighter again.

I rifled through my knowledge of West End restaurants. 'We could go to the Wolseley?' I hadn't been there either, but it seemed as good a guess as any.

'Not for dinner.' He sounded exasperated.

'Or Nobu?'

'Taxi!' Gabriel Grosse yelled at a black cab coming around the corner.

We spent the next hour riding from Covent Garden to Piccadilly then back again. At each new place Gabriel Grosse would change his mind – it wasn't what he wanted, he didn't like the look of it – and we'd jump in a taxi again.

'This town fucking sucks,' he declared after the fourth fail. By now he was playing to the crowd, a toddler high on his own mischief, and Lila and I were both laughing because it was funny and because it was required. I tried not to think about the time and the looming reality of Barbie's rushed debut.

Eventually we struck lucky in the restaurant of a five-star hotel in Mayfair. 'Order what you want,' said Gabriel Grosse, requesting a burger off the menu.

'You don't drink?' I blurted when his sparkling water arrived.

'Not anymore,' he said, his mouth full of masticated beef. He had horrible table manners, but his dark mood seemed to be lifting.

By the time we arrived at the Club the crowds had gathered outside. Gabriel Grosse took us through the main entrance, past the doorman, ignoring those trying to catch his attention.

Inside, the lobby was aglow with orange light and bright with the cooing of the lace-clad hostesses draped around the golden gun. They called out to Gabriel Grosse as we passed and went up the staircase, where faces loomed in the marmalade-coloured dark, towards the thundering noise coming from above.

Lila peeled off to get ready for the show, and I followed Gabriel Grosse to the VIP. It was still early, the Club not yet full, a cold crowd of seedy-looking men and women hunched over buckets of vodka and ice.

'How you feeling about Barbie?' Gabriel Grosse asked.

'She's a good performer,' I replied.

A wobbling circle of spotlight appeared on the curtains and a husky female voice came over the speakers. 'Okay, my babies, she's a dirty little doll, *iiiit's* Barbie!'

The track began to play, the curtains opening to reveal Barbie frozen in her box, wearing a shit-eating grin.

Her head snapped to one side as she jerked into life. Stepping from the box, elbows locked at forty-five degrees, she turned her face from left to right. Scanning the audience, I saw one or two of them smile.

Holding her hairbrush aloft, she moved her head towards the bristles in awkward, upward strokes, then tossed it to the floor, tottering back to the box to emerge clutching a Ken doll in a tiny pair of Y-fronts.

The crowd whooped as she lifted him to her face and licked him lasciviously. They were starting to warm up and Barbie, a true performer, was blossoming under their approval.

Brandishing the doll, she moved to the front of the stage where, with moves suddenly stripper-fluid, she began to grind. The audience took their cue, whistling as she tugged at the strings of her pink bikini top, wriggling her perfect behind. She whipped it off with a flourish and a cheer went up at the sight of the foam breasts, protruding like twin missiles from her chest. She hooked her thumbs beneath the fabric of the bikini bottoms and the cheering grew louder. With one movement she snatched them away to reveal . . . a flesh-coloured thong.

The sense of anticlimax sucked the energy from the room. Through the corner of my vision, I could see Gabriel Grosse's face twitching with fury.

On stage, Barbie was hamming up the drama as she pulled the Y-fronts down the Ken doll's legs, eyes widening in horror at the sight of his moulded crotch. With an anguished wail, she jabbed the doll at her own useless parts as the crowd fell about laughing.

Still wailing, she staggered to the box to retrieve the newly sprayed pink gun. Grasping it with both hands, she swung it crazily, aiming first for the audience, then at herself.

'Do it,' someone cried. 'Do it.'

As the final notes played out, Barbie stepped back inside her box. Raising the gun to her head, she screwed her eyes shut – and fired.

The gunshot blasted across the speakers; the box's window splattered with an arc of dark red blood.

There was scattered applause as Barbie slid limply to the floor, the curtains closing over the gory tableaux.

Gabriel Grosse shrugged. 'Not bad,' I heard him say.

Excusing myself, I found my way to the ladies' toilets where I shut myself in a cubicle and sat down on the seat. Through the wall, a group of girls were engaged in the manoeuvre of laying out drugs in a confined space. Listening to their giggles and sharp inhales I almost wished I could join them. There would be a certain poetry, I reflected, in having your ambitions thwarted by a sweaty latex thong.

In the neon-lit corridor, I fought my way through the crowd towards the staircase. By now, the party was crossing into the mad-hour, revellers screaming to each other at close range, chemically enhanced excitement moving through them like an electric current. At the doors to the main space, I took a breath before stepping through to the carnage within.

Gabriel Grosse was waiting for me in his private booth next to the bar, the furthest possible distance from the stage. 'If you can hear them clap from back here, you know it's a home-run,' he shouted as I squinted over the crowd.

Two girls tumbled into the booth. 'Is it okay if we sit here?' one of them asked in an accent born of old money and recent daddy issues.

With mock chivalry Gabriel Grosse gestured to the banquette next to him.

'Are you Gabriel Grosse?' I heard her say over the booming 'dong' of a large clock beginning to strike the hour.

I slipped out of the booth and stood to watch the show.

Five . . . six . . . seven . . .

The clock continued to chime, as up and down the walls rows of yellow bulbs flickered off and on.

Eight . . . nine . . . ten . . .

A beam of lemon-coloured spotlight came up on the figure of a very small man, perhaps three feet tall, in oversized top hat and tails, crouched in an alcove above the crowd.

Eleven . . . twelve.

A crunching dubstep scream blasted over the speakers and the Mad Hatter pointed to the central podium where a pretty girl in a blue dress stood, wide-eyed and blinking in the light.

Alice smiled and waved as the Mad Hatter clambered from the alcove, across tables, using members of the audience like stepping stones, until he was standing in front of her.

Bowing, he took her by the hands and danced her in a circle, before shoving her stumbling to the stage where the curtains were opening to reveal Wonderland on fire.

On a flaming golden throne, the Red Queen was sitting in red and black splendour, surrounded by her flunkeys. A latex-clad Cheshire Cat snarled as the Mad Hatter dragged Alice before the Queen, a monstrous White Rabbit breathing a stream of fire above the audience's heads.

At the foot of the throne, Alice quaked with the fear and reluctant pleasure of a skin-flick ingénue, before her tormentors hauled her to her feet once more, laughing as they yanked her to and fro, blowing clouds of powder into her face and forcing potions down her throat until her legs buckled beneath her.

Tearing at her clothes, they stripped her until she stood bare-breasted beneath the lights, then forced her to her knees before the Red Queen. The Queen's eyes rolled back as she drew the girl's head towards her crotch, the Cheshire Cat, Mad Hatter and the others melting into a bestial tangle of limbs around them as the curtains began to close . . .

I turned to say something to Gabriel Grosse at the same moment his hand shot out and landed on the girl's knee. It rested there, crouched like a tarantula. She looked up startled and I saw she'd be leaving with him that night. On his face was the same expression he'd worn earlier in the restaurant: boredom, tinged with hunger.

It was getting light when I stumbled from the Club, a blue dawn rising over the rooftops as I wobbled my way towards Chinatown.

On the corner, a street sweeper pushed his trolley past a drag queen dressed as a golden totem pole, who was attempting to fit their towering headdress and endless legs into a waiting minicab. On Wardour Street, a well-dressed man staggered on his feet as he pissed into a doorway.

Leaning against my bus stop, I closed my eyes, exhaling tequila fumes. How long had I been at the Club? It seemed like days. Underneath my tiredness, another emotion was starting to swell. It rang out triumphantly, accompanied by brass. *I've got the job. I've got the fucking job.*

Chapter 4

The corridors of the Club were painted with pigs. An elaborate mural like a Hieronymus Bosch nightmare via the Big Bad Wolf, showed dozens of them feasting at trestle tables, cannibalising their roasted contemporaries. Others flew above in hot air balloons, peering through binoculars at the giggling dancing girls below.

'They're the audience,' Lila told me. 'Gabriel calls them his dirty little piggies.'

I looked closer at the walls, picking out other characters from the Club, searching for Gabriel Grosse. What would he be doing? Roasting a pig on a pitchfork. Or perhaps a member of staff.

I added 'piggies' to the mental map I was creating of the Club. It had been two weeks since my trial and Lila had taken charge of showing me around.

'C'mon,' she said. 'Let's grab a smoke on the Beach.'

The Beach was the name of the secret roof terrace at the very top of the building, accessed via a fire escape. It had been furnished with two weather-bleached sunloungers and was used mainly, Lila said, by performers and staff for smoking and illicit sex breaks.

We stretched out in the spring sunshine and lit up, the sky above us a rich April blue. I exhaled into it, enjoying the camaraderie and sensation of being up among the rooftops.

Archie's peevish face appeared round the fire escape door.

'I've been calling you,' he said to me. 'They're about to start.'

'Who are?'

'The managers. Come on.'

I looked at Lila, who shrugged. I got up and followed Archie downstairs.

'What's happening?' I said as we hurried towards the boardroom.

'Don't you read your emails?'

'There's been about thirty today.'

The boardroom was on the third floor opposite the main office. Standing outside, I was put in mind of a humming hornets' nest as Archie rapped smartly on the door. I was aware of the identities of some of the strung-out individuals who occupied the main office during daylight hours. I knew the morose man with plum-coloured bags under his eyes was the Club's accountant, and the Sloaney girl with the endlessly chiming Blackberry, was in charge of events. The doorman with the looks of an ageing boy-band member controlled the guest list, and there were various other individuals with important-sounding titles, whose roles were not entirely clear. Today, they were arranged either side of a long table. Gabriel Grosse was sitting at one end, next to a wiry man whose eyes were hidden by light reflecting from his glasses. At the other, an enormous peroxide-blond man rested his heavy fists on the table in front of him. This was Hog, who seemed to wield some unspecified power. Opposite me was a burly guy with tattooed arms I recognised from the bar, whose sullen expression suggested a man about to undergo an unpleasant dental procedure.

40

Without preliminaries, the man in glasses began to speak in a papery monotone with an accent I couldn't place. The other managers listened respectfully though he seemed to be telling them in no uncertain terms to get their shit together. While he spoke, my eyes were drawn to the remnants of a snake tattoo on his neck.

After he'd finished, the managers took it in turns to give their account of the week gone by, Gabriel Grosse fidgeting with his phone through reports on bar spend and celebrity appearances. There was collective mirth at news of a woman who'd complained after her Chanel handbag was caught in the crossfire of one of the show's messier numbers. No, the Club would not be buying her a new one. There was excitement when it was announced a Whale would be attending the following weekend. I arranged my face into an enthusiastic smile. What the fuck was a Whale?

'So, honey.' The man in glasses turned to me. 'Are you going to tell us about the show?'

My pulse jumped to my throat. I looked to Gabriel Grosse for assistance, but he was texting furiously, scowling at his phone.

I took a breath. 'We're, uh, working on a new number for the VIP with a Drag Queen who makes a pancake and does the splits.'

Someone gave an amused snort.

'And we've got Rose in for the next couple of weeks,' Archie interjected.

There were murmurs of appreciation as I smiled through my confusion. No one had mentioned the great Rosewood would be flying in.

'What's he sticking up his arse this time?' said Hog from the far end of the table.

Gabriel Grosse looked up at the sound of his voice. 'Rose is a fucking star.'

'We're not a freak show,' said Hog. 'Where's the sex? Two models in a sixty-nine in the VIP, that's something I'd pay to watch.' He grinned around the table for support but found none. The man in glasses gazed at him for slightly too long, then continued to speak, ignoring him completely. You could almost smell the competing egos in the room, all of them hungry for a piece of the Club's power. The peroxide man's small eyes narrowed though the grin didn't leave his face. Buffoon or something more dangerous?

The meeting concluded with a rummage through the unclaimed lost property, a free-for-all that threw up all manner of treasure. I eyed a Tiffany bracelet but didn't feel bold enough to claim it for myself.

The managers began to file from the room, but as I moved towards the door, I found my path blocked by Hog.

'Hog. I run the Club.' He held out a meaty paw. 'I wanna talk to you,' he lowered his voice, 'about the show.'

'Sure.'

'Not now,' he said releasing me. 'I'll let you know when.'

In the prop cupboard, I questioned Archie on the imminent arrival of the Club's most legendary performer.

'It's been booked for months.'

'Nobody told me.'

'Oh. Weird.'

'Could you send me a list of any bookings that aren't on the wall calendar?' I kept my voice neutral.

'Fine.' He turned away and busied himself with his iPad.

'What's a Whale?' I asked him.

'Big spenders. Stupid money. This one dropped one hundred K the last time he was here.'

'*What?*'

'We'll probably have to change the show. They'll want his favourite numbers in.'

'Do they get the DJ to play his favourite songs too?'

'Yup.'

'I was joking.'

He picked up his iPad again.

'Who was that man?' I asked. 'The one in the glasses, I haven't seen him before.'

'That's the OM. Don't you know anything?'

'The who?'

'OM. He runs the company, here and in New York.'

'I thought Hog ran the company?'

'Hog?' he snorted. 'We'd be fucked.'

I'd gleaned from the gossip of Archie and Lila, of previous candidates for my job who'd disappeared as quickly as they'd arrived. I'd yet to sign a contract, my formal training conducted largely by a process of osmosis, trailing Gabriel Grosse through the building, but through observing I'd learned the main show's basic formula: two twenty-minute acts kicked off by 'Openers' featuring the MC and dancers, in which an audience member would be dragged on stage to receive mock-fellatio then doused with fake 'blood', 'piss' or 'cum'. Each act ended with a spectacular 'Closer', these were the big bangs that preceded the DJ dropping one of the latest club hits, a line of hostesses parading through the crowd with bottles of champagne topped with sparklers. All this pageantry designed to drive the audience back to the eye-wateringly expensive bar. For this reason, Closers were all-important, creating one of the best ways of cementing my position. But first I needed to understand what was required.

43

The VIP was the designated testing ground for a trainee director learning the ropes. VIP in name alone, it was used as an overflow for the main space. In reality, A-list guests seeking real privacy were given the boardroom, where they could party uninterrupted in the glare of the overhead strip lighting.

'Ruby, do you think they'll like me?' Russella said, looking anxiously at the small stage with its dirty green curtains. 'Will they think I'm shit?'

'They'll love you,' I said, knowing she was only half-joking.

Russella was a Northern drag queen with the longest legs I'd ever seen. The delight to be had watching her wrangling a camping stove while lip-synching was not to be underestimated, but now she was here I was recalling that with her genius for improvised comedy came the very real possibility of improvised chaos.

Despite my fears, the run-through went smoothly with Russella hitting every beat. The bar-backs restocking the fridges stopped to watch and laughed in all the right places. It wasn't a main stage Closer, but it was going to blow the roof off the VIP.

I checked my phone and saw Gabriel Grosse had messaged me. *Coffee? Need to show you something.*

Just tossing a pancake. Be right there, I messaged back.

I took the shortcut to the second floor via the rooftop smoking terrace. As I hurried along the corridor, my skin prickled at the sound of raised voices from the office above.

Gabriel Grosse was pacing the room, the managers cowering at their desks. None of them spoke but I noticed the accountant seemed on the verge of tears.

'Where were you?' Gabriel Grosse snapped when he saw me.

We left the Club together and walked around the corner to the Pret a Manger on Wardour Street.

'Coffee?' he demanded.

'Tea for me.'

'So English. Christ.'

'What did you want to show me?' I asked.

We sat in the window and he took out his phone and showed me a video of a yellow cartoon character I vaguely recognised.

'Make a number out of this?' He seemed in earnest.

'What are you thinking?' I said.

'Get him, like, fucking a dwarf . . . dressed as a mermaid. Or something.'

'Okay . . .'

He scowled. 'Yeah . . . it's a fucking stupid idea.'

'I don't think there are stupid ideas,' I lied. 'Only better ones.'

He seemed pacified and I congratulated myself on diverting a return to the dark side.

I'd diagnosed his outbursts, unpredictable and breathtaking in their viciousness, as the cause of the tension among the staff, my inbox home to their bickering like a chorus of Renaissance devils sent cc-all, often in the small hours of the morning. I'd psyche myself up before logging in, hoping it wasn't my turn as the focus of their wrath. Often there'd be opinions on the perceived success or failure of the previous night's show, which I chose to ignore. Despite this, I remained cocky that I was tough enough to handle them all. After years of living hand-to-mouth I was being properly paid – what did it matter if the people I worked with were rotten? To put your hand into the flame and come out unscathed. That itself was the game.

'Wanna go Burger & Lobster?' said Lila.

We were walking down Old Compton Street, seeking dinner and cocktails before the show.

'Sure,' I said.

Every few weeks Lila and the dancers would declare their allegiance to a different West End establishment. Young and beautiful, they were well-versed in dropping the Club's name to secure tables and special treatment. Burger & Lobster was the latest, its gimmick a set price of twenty pounds for either a burger or a lobster with a side order of fries. I wasn't convinced this was a particularly good deal for either, but the dancers were enthused.

'You know, Gabriel told me I'd be the next director,' Lila said when our complimentary drinks arrived.

There was a pause as I absorbed her words. 'I'm sorry,' I said carefully. 'That must be very frustrating.'

She shrugged. 'I guess he forgot.'

'We can always collaborate,' I offered. 'You're a great choreographer.'

She brightened, showing me the top row of her tiny baby's teeth. 'I'm so glad you're here.'

A pair of club kids in full regalia walked into the restaurant. They spotted our table and came over to join us.

'*Baybeee*, it's so great to see you,' Drama drawled. That night he was wearing his candy pink hair sculpted into a gravity-defying quiff.

Pathos, mirrored epaulets reflecting light from her shoulders, scooted round to sit next to me in the red PVC booth. '*Ohmygawd*, darling, how are you?' she said, air-kissing both cheeks.

From the effusiveness of their greeting, I could tell they were aware of my sudden change of fortune. It wasn't personal but that didn't stop me from enjoying my shift in net worth in the intricate social strata of London nightlife. And as we gossiped in the glow of the restaurant's warm light I had a rush of the old love I still sometimes felt for the city.

Once the remains of our dinner had been cleared away, we moved to the all-night diner on Old Compton Street for Porn Star martinis. Glancing at my phone to check the time, I saw I'd missed the debut of Russella's show and several calls from Archie.

'I've got to get back,' I told them, stumbling only a little on my heel as I stood. 'See you in there.'

White goo, like a giant cum-shot, was splattered up one side of the green velvet curtains. In front of the stage, two stagehands were busy mopping the floor.

'What happened?' I said, surveying the carnage in the VIP.

'The ironing board collapsed while Russella was mixing the batter,' said Archie, grim-faced. 'She was sliding every-where. Then the camping stove fell over.'

'Did she manage to make a pancake?'

'No pancake.'

I left the VIP, pushing my way along the corridor to the crowded smoking terrace. Squeezing through to the back, I nodded at the security guard who pulled the metal fencing aside, and stepped through to a rooftop walkway with a dazzling bird's-eye view of Soho. At the end of the walk-way, a fire-escape door was propped open with a bucket overflowing with cigarettes butts, where a couple of black-shirted ushers were smoking.

Stepping inside to the second-floor corridor, I crossed paths with the tattooed bar manager who was standing at an ironing board in his boxer shorts, engrossed in the creases of what I assumed was the missing part of his outfit. He looked up revealing exhausted green eyes and nodded without changing his expression. I gave him a weak smile in return.

The dancers' dressing room was in a den-like space, every surface bristling with lipsticks, tampons, and false eyelashes like rogue caterpillars. Shoes and abandoned stockings from their many quick-changes were scattered across the floor, the heating on permanent full-blast adding to the hot-house atmosphere of oestrogen and hairspray.

Lila was sitting at the bulb-framed mirror, applying her lipstick in the only shade of red Gabriel Grosse permitted the dancers to wear. Sitting on the floor was a nervous-looking man I recognised as a British character actor, a sheen of sweat gathering on his forehead. It was Club practice that celebrity males would be guided backstage to be 'hosted' by the dancers. However, this specimen was neither handsome nor famous enough to be much value as a celebrity scalp.

'Russella just destroyed the VIP,' I said, stepping over the actor's legs as I came in.

Lila's wide eyes opened even wider. 'What happened?'

'A slight technical hitch.'

'What did Gabriel say?'

In the mirror, I saw the eyes of the dancers shift to watch our exchange.

'He wasn't there.'

'Oh,' she breathed. 'You're lucky.' She turned back to her reflection in the mirror, and I found myself regretting I'd told her.

I went downstairs ten minutes before the main show. Standing amongst the roiling crowd, I tried not to think about Archie's report at the end of the night that was sent to all the managers. I had a hunch Gabriel Grosse didn't bother reading them but couldn't know for sure.

The bulbs lining the walls began to flicker on and off, the signal the show was about to start. The audience rose to meet it, and for a moment I was lifted off my feet, a small boat on a rising swell.

Chapter 5

I was fretting in bed when my phone rang the following morning, the name on the screen making my heart lift then plummet.

'GJ,' I answered the call.

'Darling,' said my grandmother's voice. 'How's my girl?'

'I'm . . . working.'

'What are you up to?'

'I've got a new job . . . at a nightclub. There's a show I'm directing. Dancing girls, circus . . . that sort of thing.'

She chuckled and the sound made me smile. 'You funny girl.'

'I know.' There was a pause. 'How are you?'

'Oh . . . bit dotty these days.'

'Ha. Well, me too.'

She chuckled again. 'Come and see me soon, darling.'

'Of course I will.'

'Bye bye.'

'Bye, GJ.'

We rang off and I let the hand holding the phone fall to my chest. I closed my eyes, dread crowding in as I counted the seconds until it rang again.

'Hi, GJ.'

'How's my girl?'

After our second conversation, which in every way resembled the first, had ended, I lay in bed until the urge to cry had passed. My grandmother's dementia had only become obvious the previous year, though my mother said it had been happening for some time. Now the phone calls were its constant reminder.

To me she was still my idol, a traveller from a more glamorous time, my cabin full of her: taffeta party dresses with impossible waistlines muddled in with the rest of the glad rags on the rails either side of my bed; a photograph of her as a willowy young woman, strolling through Kensington Roof Gardens, hung above the chaise upstairs. Family legend had her donning what jewellery she had to stand on a rooftop to watch the first bombs fall over London; taking a bus and a packet of sandwiches to watch the Crystal Palace burn. Like me, she had an appetite for a show; in some ways, a performer too. Born in colonial-era Kuala Lumpur, a 'Raj Orphan' parcelled off to relatives and dodgy schools, not seeing her parents for years at a time. With no official nationality and little money, she supported herself as a secretary from the age of seventeen, making the best of her charm and tenuous family connections, faking it till she made it, though I knew of at least one rich man she'd ditched weeks before the wedding. Perhaps like me, she found it hard to divine her own motives.

My wild, wonderful grandmother, who'd known the real Sally Bowles! Who once, with a twinkle in her eye, taught me the lyrics to a song from her youth: *I wish I was a fascinatin' bitch, I'd never be poor, I'd always be rich.* The one who'd always seemed to know exactly who I was and who loved me for it. Her gradual erosion like a hole carved into my chest.

I wondered what she'd make of the Club, imagined her saying, 'Darling, how ghastly!' while secretly enjoying the show. I knew she'd appreciate the high-quality whisky on the top shelf of the bar.

✻   ✻   ✻

It was early when I returned to the Club, just me and the cleaners dealing with the detritus of the night before. I went straight to the prop cupboard where I compiled a list of names. 'London performers aren't as good,' Gabriel liked to say. I'd heard it repeated at the managers' meeting and parroted by Archie and Lila, making my hackles rise. This was nonsense, of course. The Club had a reputation, and the cabaret world was small. It hadn't taken long for word of the brutal audition process to circulate, and now more seasoned performers were no longer showing up.

The first name on the list was Fancy. A cabaret superstar and the reigning Alternative Miss World, a pocket-sized, tattooed, fireball of a woman, she'd cut her teeth in the strip clubs of Seattle and had everything the Club required in terms of talent and stage presence. She was also bulletproof.

I made the call, smiling when I heard the familiar drawl at the end of the line. 'Oh *hey*, sweetie.'

'And I'll be working with you?' she demanded, once I'd explained what I had in mind.

'Yes.'

'Not Gabriel Grosse?'

'No.'

'Good. Fuck that fucking motherfucker.'

After we'd hung up, I leant my head on the cool desk. The hours between waking and dragging myself to Soho were growing shorter each day.

'Hello there.'

I looked up and was greeted by a vision in the doorway. The vision was built like a proverbial god, dressed in a flowing Indian skirt and stripy tights. A cropped vest top was stretched over an enormous pair of breasts with a flash of rippled abs below. Above this glorious cleavage was a domed bald head with a mane of purple curls, framing a long fine-boned face that was smiling.

'Hello,' I said. 'You must be Rose.'

'I was so pleased when I heard the new director was a woman,' Rose said, settling herself cross-legged on the floor. Despite her otherworldly appearance, she exuded the kindly demeanour of your favourite hippie auntie.

She'd arrived from Heathrow in the early hours of the morning at the Soho flat the Club kept specially for visiting performers, but the noise from the street had kept her awake.

'Don't worry, I'm a cranky old trannie at the best of times.' She smiled. 'I'll be just fine.'

Rose was keen to start work so we went down to the stage to look at her newest creation, a piece she'd titled 'Tea Time'.

She was crouched on a table, for which she'd donned a pair of white bloomers, when Gabriel Grosse walked in, accompanied by a slim woman carrying two yoga mats.

'It's very important you can see my fist,' Rose was saying.

'Hey, Mom,' said Gabriel Grosse.

Rose chuckled and climbed down from the table.

'You devil,' she said, embracing him.

'How are you guys getting on?'

'Oh, wonderfully.'

Gabriel Grosse introduced the Lycra-clad woman as his yoga instructor, her terrified smile displaying perfectly bleached teeth.

'Don't mind us, you carry on,' he said as she laid the mats out on the floor.

Rose climbed back on the table and the instructor began guiding Gabriel Grosse through a round of pranayama breathing. A while later, unable to resist, I glanced behind me to see him almost mirroring Rose, arse in the air in a downward-facing dog.

When I returned to the prop cupboard I was met by a stressed-looking Archie. 'We have a situation.'

'Tell me.'

'The lighting guy quit.'

'Oh well.' I wouldn't miss the Club's sullen technician, who'd made it clear he was less than impressed taking direction from a random British girl. 'When's he leaving? We'll put a call-out for a replacement.'

'No, he's *quit*. He's not coming back. Ever.'

This was indeed a situation. The Club's lighting set-up was elaborate, equipped with moving heads and strobes operated from a board at the back of the auditorium, and a manual follow-spot manned from a perch near the bar.

It was already mid afternoon, with a tech run scheduled that evening. 'Who do you usually use as backup?'

'No one . . . he was supposed to be training Reg . . .'

'Call Reg.'

Reg arrived an hour later, the follow-spot kid now promoted to lighting designer. I looked him over, twenty if a day, with messy blond hair like a freshly hatched chick.

'Do you know how to use the desk?' I asked him.

'Sort of . . . a lot of the numbers are pre-programmed; you just need to cue them.'

'Hope you're ready for your debut.'

Reg wasn't ready but we had no other choice. The dancers arrived, annoyed at being called in early, and we set about working through the cues for the Openers that night. Rose was helpful, offering to switch her numbers to ones that happened largely out in the crowd and, somehow, we limped through the tech, finishing fifteen minutes before doors. There was no time to dash out for something to eat, so I ordered chips from the kitchen on the lower level manned by a bored Chinese chef, whose presence had something to do with a loophole in the Club's entertainment licence.

I had a shot at the bar to steady my nerves, then went to check on the performers preparing to go on stage. A disconcerting experience, sticking my head around the dressing-room door and watching them startle when less than a month ago I was applying the same paint to my face in some other backstage mirror. Rose was there, in tartan skirt, army boots and fright wig. She grinned, displaying a mouth of blacked-out teeth, and I wished them all luck.

Gabriel Grosse had referred to Rose as a 'cornerstone' of the Club – the Closer to end all Closers, though tonight she'd be opening the show. Standing in the crowd, I tingled with anticipation while trying to project an air of hostility to discourage the men who circled like flies.

The lights started flickering on and off, the spotlight swinging towards a commotion at the back of the room, announcing the entrance of Rose. And as I watched her detonate the room like a human bomb, I understood everything.

Mornings had grown narrower in the weeks I'd been at the Club. Seconds of coffee, stumbling half-asleep to the bus, then back in the prop cupboard nursing a hangover. My new state of normal.

I was squinting in the glare of the computer screen, typing out an email, when I was interrupted by Rose looking panicked.

'My wig for Love. I can't find it.'

I blinked. 'Are you sure?'

'I think I left it back in New York.' Rose's hands were trembling.

I pulled myself together. 'What do you need?'

She described the wig in question. A shake-and-go from the fancy dress shop wasn't going to cut it.

'I know someone who might be able to help,' I said and made a call to Kristian.

'I can do it,' he said. 'If you can get the hair.'

I conveyed the news to Rose. 'I know a place, it's twenty minutes on the Tube.'

'I'm not great with directions . . .'

I texted Archie that I'd be gone for the afternoon and together with Rose, who donned a silver leather jacket for the journey, set off through the back streets of Soho towards Oxford Circus.

We got on the Victoria line, bound for Finsbury Park and the hairy mile of wholesale wig and weave shops beloved by the city's cabaret performers, drag queens and wig makers. As we pulled north, Rose was calm, and we began to ease into our adventure.

'I don't really know the city outside of Soho,' she confided, as we sat side by side on the Tube.

'You should come and visit my boat,' I told her. 'It's the most beautiful view in London.'

'A barge?'

'No, military. A World War II motor torpedo boat converted in the sixties.'

'How wonderful. I've always considered charming living arrangements to be a sign of a nice inner life.'

Rose told me she lived in Manhattan at the Chelsea Hotel. Raised Jewish, she was now a Yogi of some thirty years, and when not performing ran a successful antique restoration business.

At Finsbury Park, we spent a marvellous hour browsing the row of shops offering a bewildering selection in every colour and style, Rose drilling the stunned proprietors on the quality of their goods. I admired the way she moved through the world, her serenity carrying her above the stares of passers-by, her gracious manner prompting the same response in return. Eventually, we found several bags of human hair in the correct Titian-hue and a cheap wig to use as a base, as Kristian had instructed.

It was dark by the time we returned to Soho, so we went for dinner in Chinatown. Over XO dumplings, Rose told me of her life before the Club, her first taste of performing as a teenage magician working in a children's prison. To my surprise, her eyes misted over at the mention of a well-known cabaret performer who'd recently transitioned. 'She's lucky. It wasn't easy when I was her age, and we had no NHS. She's still young enough for the treatments to make a difference to her face.'

'I'm sorry,' I said, because what else was there to say? How would it feel to be a woman forced to live your life trapped forever in a halfway place?

She smiled. 'No use in dwelling. These days I just tend my garden, you know?'

Rose's garden. I pictured it as a place of stories and the lessons of a life most could never conceive, but a place of peace. There are those who choose a career on stage for its flexible hours and dubious perks, but for others it can be a way of communicating truths about who you are, the world as you find it. Of teaching those who in other circumstances might never listen.

She told me of the Emirates sheikh, who came to the Club every night Rose was in town, always with a large group in tow, for the purpose of demonstrating 'everything wrong with Western culture'.

'But he keeps coming back,' I said.

'Yes,' said Rose, a twinkle in her eye. 'He does.'

There was a funny smell on board the boat when I got home that evening, where I found Kristian using tweezers to apply rhinestones to the green military jacket he'd sewn over the weekend.

I watched anxiously as he examined Rose's hair with a critical eye. 'Is it the right stuff?'

'I can make it work,' he said, fitting the wig base over the mannequin head.

I collapsed on the chaise and exhaled. 'Well, thank fuck for that.'

I watched as he busied himself with his needles, hook and thread. Adept with a sewing machine as he was with a hammer and saw, there were few things Kristian couldn't make.

'You should come and work at the Club,' I said.

He looked up. 'Do they need someone?'

'Desperately. I'd have to sell it to them though.'

'That would be amazing,' he said softly. Lately, Kristian had been surviving between auditions by assisting the Cat with his various pursuits. And while he was grateful for the work, I knew he found the Cat's working methods emotionally exhausting.

'I'll do my best,' I told him. 'By the way, what's that horrible fucking smell?'

The smell was coming from the kitchen. I identified its source as coming from my vegetable steamer simmering on the stove. Peering beneath the lid, I let out a yelp. At the bottom of the pan were three tiny, ravaged faces, half-submerged in what had been half-boiled from the bones. The sockets of their empty skulls seemed to gaze mournfully back at me.

'Felicity?' I called, unable to keep the anger out of my voice.

'*Yeees?*' came the innocent reply.

'What is this?'

The sound of her door sliding open. She appeared wearing a pair of pink satin pyjamas, her hair wrapped in a towel.

'Ooo,' she cooed. 'Those are just my squirrel heads. I'm giving them a clean.'

'But why are they in my vegetable steamer?'

Felicity's eyes seemed to double in size. 'I'm sorry, dear, I didn't think you'd mind.'

'Of course I bloody mind,' I growled. 'I should throw them in the Thames.'

I stomped to my cabin and lay face down on the bed. I had a vague memory of Felicity telling me of her ambition to become a taxidermist, which I'd taken with a pinch of salt. Recently she'd been making declarations about her next career move, from 'milliner' to 'feminist porn director', which proved only theoretical in practice. Felicity was a fine performer, a triple-threat of Clara Bow face, pillowy curves, and natural comedic timing, but there was simply less work these days – or more performers prepared to work for less. And while I was sympathetic, the squirrel skulls were just the latest in a series of disgusting incidents to have recently befallen the boat. The previous week, someone had knocked over the ironing board, disconnecting the socket to the fridge. We realised only after a red-yellow goo started oozing from the freezer compartment; an unholy mixture of vanilla ice cream, defrosted meat, and half an ounce of speed that Maciek had attempted to salvage. This came hot on the heels of a party during which the vacuum drainage system had gone down, causing the toilet to overflow just metres from my bed. It was all too much. Other people didn't live like this. I was tired of the cold and the damp and the leaks, the revolting oven; of mouldy clothes and hearing people pissing through my cabin wall. Cheap wine, grime in the bathtub and never feeling clean. Of broken sleep, the floor thumping overhead. Broken electronics, broken glass, broken taps and rotting wood. The feeling of your life decomposing around you. Things were changing for me, but I knew without being told that Gabriel Grosse would be unlikely to let Felicity's lovely body anywhere near his stage.

I got up from the chaise and went downstairs and knocked on her cabin door.

'Come in,' said a small voice from inside.

I slid the door open. Felicity's cabin had been decorated as a boudoir in shades of jade green and pink, with kinky detailing when you looked a little closer. A gold-winged phallus – an award she'd received for her hosted screenings of vintage pornography – took pride of place.

Felicity was in bed, her laptop balanced on her knees. She looked at me sorrowfully. 'I'm sorry I used your pan.'

'I'm sorry I was grumpy,' I said. 'I'm wound quite tight at the moment.'

She set her laptop aside and flipped up the edge of her duvet. I walked over and joined her beneath the covers of the narrow bed. We snuggled down, and for a while we were silent.

'Things are going to get better,' I said.

She gave me a squeeze in reply.

'What were you watching?'

'Something rather special.'

'Oh, yes?'

'Ever heard the rumours about Brando starring in blue movies?'

'*No.*'

'Care to watch?'

'That's the second best offer I've had all week.'

The evening before Tea Time's debut, I sought Rose out in the dressing room. Her stage preparations were elaborate. Before applying her make-up, she pulled the skin back from her face using an intricate system of tape and invisible threads, before inserting a special butt plug to prepare herself for what was to come. Rose's numbers often featured what she termed 'body tricks', involving an alarming degree of self-harm inflicted on her still-intact cock and balls or internally via her rectum. One number saw her eating chocolate pudding from the bowl of a toilet before penetrating herself with a toilet brush. I'd seen her set her cock on fire after wrapping it in paper towels, and nail her testicles to her perineum with a staple gun. There were those who might find it horrific, but Rose approached her performances from a conceptual point of view, drawing on her past work with sex workers and drug addicts during the AIDS epidemic of the eighties, which she'd survived though many of her friends were dead. 'My numbers are all aspects of me,' she explained. 'Or something I've lived through.' To the Club's audience of drunk City boys, Russian oligarchs, coked-up celebrities, and club kids on the hustle, they were the last word in entertainment.

I fought my way to the middle of the room, my preferred spot for watching the show. As always, the dance floor was an apocalypse of ear-splitting noise and deranged lighting, hostesses gyrating in alcoves set into the walls as the crowd staggered and heaved.

Someone caught my arm and I turned to see a man with eyes that had been boiled. I shook him off. 'I'm working.'

He stepped closer. 'Are you a hostess?'

'I'm the director.'

He opened his mouth then faltered. 'I used to be a creative,' he said hopefully.

I turned away and fixed my eyes on the stage.

Athena, the Club's statuesque MC appeared under the spotlight, in a glittering corset.

'And now, my babies,' she purred in her honeyed Southern drawl. 'You are *not* ready for this. It's my NYC homegirl Rose, in *Tea Tiiiiime.*'

The curtains opened to reveal a derelict Victorian garret bathed in darkness but for the light from a candelabra held by an agitated figure hunched behind a large table, absorbed in tossing things over their shoulder: napkins, linens and knickers. Searching for something.

The figure straightened and the audience got their first look at Rose in a corseted gown, her frantic face lit by candlelight. She looked rather beautiful in her Titian curled wig, like a painting by Modigliani.

Rushing to a small table that held a stack of books, she slammed the candelabra down, rifling through the books, hurling them to the floor until she found what she was looking for. Snatching up a silver hand mirror, she gazed as if mesmerised by her own reflection, her expression shifting to one of distress as she cast it away, tearing open the gown to reveal her breasts marked with dark red gashes, masterfully drawn in stage paint.

Reaching behind her, she grasped something from a tray on the large table, light glinting off the blade of the large chef's knife as she drew its point deeply across her chest, a hand stealing down to grasp the place between her legs even as her face contorted with pain. Rummaging beneath her skirts, she reached inside the split in her bloomers to extract a dripping tampon, blood coursing down her wrist as she brought it close to her mouth, somewhere between desire and disgust.

Tossing the tampon aside, her attention moved to the large object at the far side of the table, obscured by a black dust sheet.

Struggling, she dragged the thing to the front of the stage, tearing the sheet away to reveal a frail man in a tattered black evening jacket and white shirt stained with red. He was naked from the waist down, tied to a chair, bound and helpless. This was Lavinia, an elderly Cockney drag queen, who could usually be found haunting the corridors like a gorgeous moth in decaying Miss Havisham drag.

There was madness in Rose's eyes as she grasped the knife once more, pointing it at the man then stabbing it into the table.

No . . . The man shook his head as she picked up a silver platter, pleading as she wiped it clean and placed it between his legs. She towered over him, a fork now in hand. *No* . . . *no* . . . The man howled as Rose dived for his crotch, appearing to pinion his cock while he screamed in agony.

Using the platter to catch the bloody flow, she carried it

ceremoniously to the table, thrusting her hand in, smearing it this way and that, until it was fully red.

She unhooked her gown and let it drop to the floor. *No . . . no . . .* The man whimpered as Rose scrambled on top of the table to crouch on all fours. Her arse to the audience, she parted her bloomers to reveal her muscular backside and the puckered brown knot at the centre.

Hand held high, the wet red gleaming in the spotlight, Rose turned to lock eyes with the man who shook his head: *Please don't.* Then, with exquisite timing, she began to push her clenched fist inside her arsehole, the room descending into screams as her forearm disappeared almost to the elbow.

Holding eye contact, Rose started slowly, purposefully, to fist herself . . . gently at first, then harder.

Rose had told me that Tea Time was about hysteria and the torment of disembodied desire, inspired by her experiences taking the hormone oestrogen that had given her sexual impulses biologically impossible for her to fulfil. Looking at the crowd, I wished I could take a photo of their faces. If the barometer for what makes successful theatre is how much and how intensely a piece makes an audience feel, then Tea Time was off the scale. They were terrified, and it was thrilling to see these spoiled urbanites who'd come looking for kicks and a taste of the wild side having their minds ripped apart by the spectacle of Rose's extraordinary sorrow.

When it was over, Rose climbed down from the table, and once more approached the man swooning in pain and fear. Leaning down, she shoved his head to the side, the knife held close to his face as the audience, mad with anticipation, waited for the final blow.

At the last possible moment of unbearable tension, Rose

leaned in and kissed him tenderly on the lips. It was a gesture so unexpected and sweet that you felt it deep inside you. As she pulled away, he turned to the audience before his eyes rolled back, rapture on his smiling face.

Gently, Rose laid him down and covered him with the dust sheet. Picking up the mirror once more, she resumed admiring her reflection, toying with her hair as the curtains began to close.

There was a shell-shocked pause before applause like white noise rushed forward in a wave. I looked around at the faces of the audience distorted in horrible parodies of mirth, eyes bulging, their laughter too loud in their eagerness to show just how disgusted, how *grossed-out* they were.

And it seemed to me then, in Rose's depiction of the addictive nature of cruelty, that here was a strange grain of truth.

Chapter 6

Here is the Club, a doorway in an ugly alley. No sign outside. Were it not for the crowd clamouring on the wrong side of the velvet rope, you'd hurry your step as you passed, seeking wider, better-lit streets. The doorman, sour-faced, scans the line for pretty women, monied suits, a scattering of club kids for colour. To queue is to have already failed. Cooling in the alley with the rest of the unchosen is to admit you are not enough, though some of you may 'do', eventually.

You step through. The doorman does not touch his own velvet rope. Inside, all is warmth and shadows and smiling creatures waiting to greet you with nipples and lace. Up the curving stairs, the lights grow dimmer as the bass gets louder. People stumble past, a couple grind against a wall. Through a set of doors, a body shock of sound, blue-black darkness and thrashing limbs. Every sense assaulted, the lights pure violence. You move forward and are swallowed. Now is the time to submit, your boundaries and your borders mean nothing here. Skin against skin, you feel the edges of yourself dissolve. Faces turn towards you, eyes searching – everyone here is searching – then look away again. The forgetting is immediate. It isn't you they want.

Something is happening, your eyes follow the concentration of movement and energy. On stage a sack-faced monster with a flaming strap-on is terrorising a girl in a baby doll nightie, whose bedroom is on fire.

You wonder for a moment what all this means, but it's eclipsed by the notion that this is the party you've been waiting for all your life. Other wonders appear. An acrobat balances on a pole supported only by her chin, bending backwards to fire an arrow with her feet. A woman inserts a pair of shears inside her, blood flowing from between her thighs.

They are gone before you have time to understand. You battle to the bar and hand your money over gladly. This is not a place to be sober. Above you, someone is dancing, legs impossibly long, her midnight limbs seem to stretch the length of the room. You want to dance with her, but she looks straight through you. The night is endless, until it ends.

You find yourself outside, blinking in the cool blue light. Dirty, satisfied and spent, the rising day a horror, skin sticky with a post-porn glow. Tomorrow, when it comes, you will not recall this feeling, only fragments and a lurking shame, and pride in the knowledge that you were there, part of it all.

The Club doors opened at eleven, when the first guests began to trickle in, and by midnight it was full. Who came varied depending on the night. I preferred Wednesdays and Thursdays when the atmosphere was less aggressive, lighter on blundering bankers, the club kids genuinely excited to be there. On these nights, the Club gave the enterprising among them their own table and a bottle of vodka, in exchange for populating the front row with photogenic friends. Celebrities and beautiful women were also prominently seated – essential window dressing to offset the male-heavy crowd. The West End regulars were a curiosity, professional partygoers on first-name terms with the door staff of central London. Flashily dressed and cocaine confident, I never understood what they did during daylight hours. Then there were Trustafarians and those with famous parents, and of course there were the Whales, those most rare and valuable of creatures, who arrived from far-flung places to indulge in the Club's particular delights. On the occasion of a Whale-sighting, the Club existed for them alone, an elaborate play in which every member of staff had a part. If the Club got it right, then the Whale would stay – and pay – perhaps return the following night. The VIP tables had no set price – the Club decided what each client could afford. A Whale might spend thousands reserving the front row that the previous night had housed a gaggle of club kids pissed on free booze. Backstage – bedlam. Bodies in every stage of undress squashed together in the dressing room amidst teasing and gossip and bits being taped. Performers appearing in the prop cupboard with requests for lube, a sterile safety pin, white noise; Archie briefing his stagehands like an angel-faced Hitler Youth in demi-drag. The dancers whispering behind the door of their private sanctum, while hostesses with regional accents bantered with the barbacks in the corridor outside. All of this building like champagne shaken in a bottle until it was time for the party to begin.

Half an hour before showtime, I was up on the Beach avoiding it all, taking advantage of the first minutes I'd had to myself since midday.

Exposed in the cold night air, I shivered. Below me, I could hear the drunken voices of those crammed onto the smoking terrace. For them, it was the start of the night.

I tried not to think about the long week ahead. Taking a final, long drag of my cigarette, I exhaled into the starless sky.

Turning to go, I saw that something was wrong. The fire door, which had been propped open, was closed.

I walked over to it and pushed. It didn't budge. I grasped the handle and rattled. Fumbling for my phone, I saw several missed calls from Archie. I pressed return call, then tried Lila. Nothing.

I banged with my fist, knowing that no one would hear, and banged harder anyway.

'Really?' I said as my skin tingled with the first cold drops of rain.

Wrapping my arms around my shoulders I hunched down on one of the sunloungers. There was nothing to do but wait.

A shriek of laughter pealed out over the night. Whoever they were, they'd be missing the show too.

There was a clunking sound behind me. I looked around to see the fire door opening, followed by a glimmering of pink sequins as Lavinia stepped onto the Beach.

She looked at me in surprise. 'Hello, luvvie,' she said. 'You locked out?'

I stood up. 'I was.'

'Someone moved the bucket.' She tutted, bending down to prop it against the door.

I looked at the bucket heavy with sand. Lavinia was right. It couldn't have moved on its own.

She straightened up with a wince and I found myself wondering how old she was beneath her paint.

'No harm done,' she said. 'You best get warm. Go and get yourself a nice brandy.'

69

I gave her a kiss on her powdery cheek as I headed for the stairs. 'Thanks for rescuing me.'

'Mind your back now,' she said, her words following me as I hurried towards the sound of the first Opener drifting up from the stage. Would someone lock me out deliberately? Though some of the staff weren't exactly friendly, I hadn't made an enemy as far as I knew.

But as I cast my mind back over the weeks I'd been at the Club, I found I wasn't so sure.

Bzzzzz. A noise like an angry wasp penetrated the heavy blanket of my sleep. *Bzzzzz.*

I grasped for the thing vibrating on my bedside shelf, forcing my eyes to open, reality fighting its way through the haze. I was on the boat. It was day. But what day was it?

Holding my phone in front of my face, I recognised an American dial code. 'Hello?' I croaked.

'So, honey.'

My stomach lurched as I recognised the clipped tones of the OM. Of all the staff I'd met, he was the only one I found genuinely unnerving. Quiet of voice and footstep, he didn't so much arrive as materialise, dispatching orders which on closer inspection seemed almost nonsensical – a weird hybrid of Orwellian Newspeak and business terminology. This in contrast to the marauding creature he became at night, eyes bulging and lips foam-flecked. He'd returned to the US not long after I'd arrived. Why was he calling me now?

'Are you there?' he said.

'Yes, I'm here,' I rasped through lips dry as dust.

'I've been reading the show report from last night.'

'Oh . . .'

'I want to ask you a question.' The OM spoke slowly as if talking to a child. 'Given the chance, what would you have done differently?'

I winced, remembering. 'There were too many pissing numbers. There was piss in the finale of the Opener, then Rose pissed all over the audience at the end of Act One. And there was piss again in the Opener of the second act.'

'Very good. You can't have two numbers featuring urination back to back. And you can't have three urination numbers in one show.'

'Too much piss.'

'Exactly.'

After we'd rung off, I stared stupidly at the screen. I tried to recall if I'd discussed the Openers' endings with Lila, but my memory was foggy from the whisky I'd consumed. I checked the time. Three hours until Fancy's tech. I sat up, released a hacking cough and swung my legs out of bed.

I wobbled down the corridor, the hull creaking as it keeled from side to side. 'Does it rock?' was the question asked without fail by those discovering I lived on a boat. 'Yes,' I'd say. 'She does.' The boat rocked, gently unless a larger vessel was passing, groaning as she rose like an ageing beast woken from slumber, water sloshing inside the bilge, wooden planking braced against the pressure. Though I'd always felt she was happiest afloat.

In the kitchen amidst the clinking of swinging crockery, I put the kettle on and gulped down a pint of water. Where was everybody? Once, I'd rarely found myself alone on the boat but now I often woke to a ghost ship. It was one of several ways my life's rhythm was shifting. At the start I'd pitied those staff whose lives seemed to revolve entirely around the Club. But here I was, one of them.

My skull was throbbing, and I contemplated stealing one of Maciek's codeine pills, then decided against it. I opened the fridge and found nothing but some out-of-date milk and photographic film. I'd buy a sandwich on the way in.

That night in the dressing room, I sat with Fancy while she instructed me on how to plait her hair around a metal climbing carabiner.

'Like this?'

'Tighter.'

'I don't want to hurt you.'

'Oh, sweetie.' She smiled behind her paint. 'It's going to hurt whatever you do.'

Tonight, this plait would be the only thing standing between Fancy and a nasty fall, so I was anxious to do it right. An ancient circus skill, hair-hanging was a dying art. Fancy had taught herself the technique hanging from the stairwell of her Dalston flat. Aside from being extremely painful, few modern aerialists had tresses long enough, but Fancy, who'd never let anyone cut hers, had a glossy black curtain that fell almost to her knees.

'How do I secure the end?' I said when I'd finished.

A young stagehand with a towering high top, stuck his head around the door. 'Okay, sexy gorgeous people, this is your twenty-minute call.'

Eerily calm, her face painted in a Butoh-style mask, Fancy took a tiny sip from her glass of champagne.

At ten minutes to curtain, the performers and stage crew trooped down the small flight of stairs to the back of the stage. Archie was wearing the headset he used to cue the sound and lighting, and a tight-fitting tuxedo over bare chest and pearls.

The heavy curtains were drawn, blocking out the crowd on the other side of the velvet. On stage, the performers psyched themselves up, dancing, stretching and mock humping each other, Lila and the dancers dressed as slutty schoolgirls, ready for the Opener.

At five minutes to curtain, Athena made her regal entrance, diamanté-studded microphone in hand. 'Okay, babies,' she purred. 'Let's go fuck shit up.'

The performers whooped, stagehands scattering to the wings, and I ducked through the gap at the side of the curtain to take my place in the audience. They were restless tonight, a feeling of impatience in the room.

The spotlight started to swing across the curtains, Athena's voice over the mic.

Showtime.

My heart was in my mouth during the first Opener. It was over in a flash, the dancers scampering from the stage in a cloud of fake cocaine. Then Athena said Fancy's name and the lights went down, the curtains opening to the sound of unearthly chanting and the hypnotic beat of a kettle drum.

Fancy was standing at the back of the stage, a dancer on either side as her inscrutable handmaidens.

Slowly, they walked forwards, Fancy's white kimono trailing, her grave face motionless beneath the tight topknot. The drums began to beat in double time as they reached the edge of the stage.

Fancy extended her arms as the dancers untied her scarlet obi and slipped the kimono from her body, leaving her naked, bathed in beams of dancing white light, her many black tattoos on full display.

The ushers held back the crowd as in stately procession Fancy and the dancers stepped from the stage towards the

73

central podium. I walked alongside, alert to any interference by drunken punters but they remained respectfully at bay.

The winch began to lower as they arrived at the podium, stopping a few inches above head height. One dancer held it steady, the other attaching the carabiner concealed inside Fancy's hair.

Giving the pre-planned signal with her arms, Fancy cued the winch and began to lift, the skin around her eyes stretching as she rose, first to her tiptoes, then slowly into the air. She ascended towards the central dome, turning slowly, her face perfectly composed, moving her limbs into elegant shapes, the audience gawping at her small strong body suspended for their entertainment.

Lowering again to the podium, Fancy took a short circular run, lifting again in a graceful curve, ending in a pirouette beneath the glowing dome that changed from blue, to pink, to red.

I found myself studying the faces of the audience, their expressions revealing a spectrum of emotion from disgust to awe, and at the centre of it all was Fancy, their eyes burning whatever meaning they found into the surface of her skin. What a rush! What power she had then.

Before the final lift, Fancy brought her hands to the chopsticks decorating her hair, jamming them into the blood bags secreted inside. Dark red-black streaks cascaded down her face and body as she raised to the ceiling once more. At the highest point, she held her arms tight to her chest, centrifugal force causing her to spin faster, faster, faster . . .

Cut to black.

In the dark, a grin spread across my face as the applause hit my system like a drug.

*   *   *

Fancy was standing naked in the dressing room, fake blood trickling down her legs.

'Was it okay?' she asked.

'You killed it,' I laughed. 'How's your head?'

'It fucking hurts.' But I could see she was pleased.

Archie stuck his head round the dressing-room door. 'Amazing,' he said. 'Well done.'

'Nice job on the winch,' I told him. 'The timing was perfect.'

He looked surprised, nodded once, and disappeared again.

'I'm going to shower,' Fancy announced.

'Want another champagne?'

'Please, sweetie.'

Making my way to the back of the room the crowd seemed different somehow. Tonight, they looked beautiful. Faces appeared as if lit from within, attraction flaring as gazes connected then broke away again, my skin crackling with all the secret signals of the dance floor.

At the bar, the tattooed bar manager stood me next to him while he mixed me a margarita.

'*Ghost in the Shell*,' he shouted, handing over my drink. 'One of the finest anime movies ever made, in my humble opinion.'

The music had been Fancy's choice, but I wasn't about to tell him that.

'You're an anime fan?' I shouted back.

'Oh yes,' he grinned. 'I'm a total geek. Don't be fooled by the tattoos, it's only bravado to compensate for my tiny penis.'

'It's not the size that counts, or so I've heard.'

'Exactly, and mine is small but deadly. Like a bullet.'

75

'Liar, liar.'

He grinned. 'Enzo, by the way.'

'Ruby.'

'I know your name, *Madame* director.'

On the other side of the counter, I could hear people talking about Fancy's Hair Hang. *Did you see? Was it real?* My elation was climbing, extending across the room, feeding on their excitement, higher and higher. I spent the rest of the night charging through the backstage corridors, glass in hand. On the smoking terrace, Calypso the events manager, introduced me as *our fabulous director* to the bemused daughter of a Rolling Stone, a hostess demonstrating her approval by spanking me with her riding crop. When, finally, the Club closed and the last of the drunks had been herded into the street, the performers and staff gathered in the main room under the houselights, sparking up cigarettes and cracking bottles, applauding Reg the spotlight kid when he filled his mouth with gas from a lighter and set it on fire. Sometime after that, I found myself on the Beach with Lavinia, smoking her liquorice roll-ups as the sky grew mauve above us. Friday morning announced itself, workers clip-clopping on their way to offices in the street below, others rolling up the shutters of cafes to crank up the coffee machines, dealers of more potent drugs melting from clubs into waiting cabs headed for after-parties all over the city. I would be late today, I decided, but it was time to go home. I bid Lavinia goodnight and tottered off across the roof, stopping only briefly to let the warm air from a vent blow my skirt around my waist, Marilyn-style.

Walking along the Embankment, a pink dawn was breaking above a low tide. I paused to watch the herons picking their way across the mudflats. I loved returning to the boat at first light for the silent Thames, the impossibility of peace in the centre of the city.

My morning reverie was interrupted by my phone.

'Hey, kid.' Gabriel Grosse sounded tinny and far away.

'Oh hey!' I suppressed a hiccup.

He laughed softly. 'Just finished work?'

'I'm walking by the river.'

'Going for a swim?'

'Going home to my boat.'

'Ha. Course you live on a boat. Does it rock?'

'Yes, it does.'

Then he said: 'Hair Hang. That's a killer number.'

'Were you there? I didn't see you.'

'You're doing a great job.'

'Thank you.'

'I had some thoughts to make it bang even more. You got time?'

I stifled a yawn and walked towards a wrought iron bench next to the river wall.

'Sure,' I said, and sat down.

Chapter 7

The world would end on my thirtieth birthday, or so the internet said. The Rapture was coming – the last Judgement when God's elect would ascend to heaven. And while no one on the boat minded if they made the grade, it was, we all agreed, an excellent theme for a party. The dress code: *Apocalypse Wow.*

We spent the day battening down the hatches, shoving anything breakable into dusty corners and rolling back the rugs. I'd decided to decorate with dry ice, borrowing a smoke machine from the Club with the help of Reg who'd sneaked it out the stage door. I was lying on the floor attempting to locate the plug socket behind the junk beneath the chaise, when the Cat appeared, an enormous white box in his arms.

'Kitty,' I smiled, pleased to see him.

'Awright.'

I got to my feet, sneezing twice. 'Sorry, dusty down there. What's in the box?'

'It's, uh, cake.'

I opened the box and peered at the chocolate and cream confection inside. 'Thank you,' I said, and kissed him. I didn't care that the cake might have been stolen. That he'd made the connection between 'birthday' and 'cake' was enough.

'I've got speakers,' he said, 'but I might need, uh, help.'

I rounded up the crew and together we trooped down the pontoons to where the van was parked on the loading bay. I whooped with laughter when I saw the sound system, battered and vast as a Notting Hill Carnival rig.

'They're not going to fit,' Kristian said, when we'd managed to manoeuvre the great wooden stacks to the foot of the gangway, where we stood contemplating the front door.

'What about over the roof?' I said.

'There's no way.'

'Safety first,' said Maciek, who loved it when things went wrong.

'I think I'll put the kettle on,' Felicity said and disappeared inside.

Despite his misgivings, Kristian was persuaded to join Maciek and me in hauling the speakers across the roof. The Cat stood impassively on the foredeck, a roll-up dangling from his lips as we toppled them into his outstretched arms.

Once they were safely on board, I left Kristian and the Cat setting up and went downstairs to change into my costume. A chainmail skirt slit up both sides with a matching bikini, and blond mohawk with a crest of Barbie legs, made specially by Kristian for the occasion. In the bathroom mirror, I carefully pinned it onto my head and stood back, delighted with the final effect. It was an outfit to see in the End of the World.

In the managers' meeting, Fancy's Hair Hang had been declared a 'homerun' by even the frostier members of staff. I'd signed my contract not long after, in the boardroom with only Gabriel Grosse and the OM present.

'You own my soul now,' I said, inking my name on the unfamiliar document.

'Oh, we don't need that,' said Gabriel Grosse.

Taking advantage of my new-found favour, I'd requested the weekend off to scout some new acts. This, I reasoned, was not entirely untrue – there would be a lot of performers at the party.

The decks had been set up in the living room next to the speakers that dominated an entire wall. When we turned them on, the windows rattled in their frames.

I paced around the kitchen, skittish with nervous energy.

'Shall we have some champagne?' said Felicity, easing out a cork.

'They're here,' called Maciek from upstairs.

Hidden behind the speakers, my skull vibrating with the obscene levels of bass, I pressed the button on the smoke machine and white fog filled the living room. The spirit of mischief jiggering in my veins, I pressed again, sending another jet of chemical haze to obscure the dancers until they were only visible as interruptions in the skittering laser beams. Beneath me the floor bounced and buckled, and I wondered if this would be the night it finally gave way.

Keeping my head down, I crawled towards the hubbub coming from below. Downstairs, the kitchen was rammed wall to wall with apocalyptic visions wreathed in smoke from a hundred cigarettes. Next to the fridge, Pris from *Blade Runner* was having an intense conversation with a woman in a bra made of taxidermy pigs' heads. They were interrupted by the dramatic entrance of a long-legged creature in an orange prison jumpsuit and elephant's trunk, lowering itself through the hatch in the ceiling. At the counter, a gang of *Warriors* had formed a percussive trio, drumming on wine bottles and saucepans with cutlery, while in the corner the Cat quietly nursed a nosebleed.

I found myself cornered by an Edwardian rent boy I didn't remember inviting. I focused on his ruddy complexion while he gave me unsolicited advice about the Club. Why did aristocrats always have such lovely skin?

'Just enjoy it, darling,' he said, pulling on his miniature cigar.

'Mmm,' I said. Perhaps it was dietary?

Nearby, Russella was describing taking ayahuasca to a girl wearing an enormous vagina for a hat.

'Do you feel different now?' the girl was saying.

'It's quite subtle really, but I'm making deeper connections with guys on Grindr.'

'I like Gabriel, you know,' the rent boy was saying. 'Lot of fun. Shame he's sober now really.'

'I'll be right back,' I said.

I made my way along the corridor clogged with staggering people. At the far end, Maciek had staked out the toilet, guarding the entrance like a drug-addled Sphinx, and judging by the moans from behind the door the bathroom was currently in use. Opposite was a row of cupboards built into the wall. I opened the sliding door of one.

'Hello, bunny,' Felicity said, peering out from between the coats.

'Hello,' I said climbing in to join her. 'I didn't know you were in here.'

'Come and snuggle. But mind those bloody Barbie legs.'

I squeezed in next to her and we sat in the dark listening to the chaos from above.

'It's a pretty good party,' I said.

'Is that why you're in here?'

'I'm laying low till everyone stops asking about the Club.'

'Ah, because now you are the Queen of Soho with the power to bestow guest list.'

'I'm not sure I like it.'

'You *love* it.'

'Anyway, I'm not – Gabriel Grosse is.'

'The Queen?'

'More the Prince of Darkness.'

'Grand High Cunt?'

There was a crash in the kitchen.

'Blimey,' said Felicity.

'Maciek isn't letting anyone into the loo and the Cat's covered in blood.'

'I shouldn't worry.'

'I'm thirty, Fee. I'm not sure I pictured it like this.'

'Hiding in a cupboard dressed as Tina Turner?'

'Oh, fuck off.'

There was another crash, this time accompanied by a roar and a round of applause.

'I've been thinking,' Felicity said. 'I'm giving up cabaret.'

'Oh yes?'

'Did you know, if you put yoghurt and moss in a blender, you can paint it on a wall in any design you like, and the moss will grow back the same shape?'

'I did not know that.'

'I'm going to be an avant-garde gardener. The overheads are low – yoghurt is cheap.' I couldn't see her face but could sense her drug-addled fervour in the dark.

'You've really thought it through.'

'Oh yes.'

What makes a great party? There are mysterious factors at play. The people, music, drugs and weather can all play a part. Performing had taught me that sometimes it's the dullest parties that look most impressive in the pages of magazines; throwing money at something is no guarantee. Even after years and thousands of nights I did not have the answer, but as the boat continued to fill with freakishly dressed revellers, I knew the stars had aligned in my favour. As the night raged on, I felt everywhere at once, time fracturing into a tickertape of edited highlights. A vision of myself, seen from outside, lying on the floor pretending to be a hoover while Maciek held onto my legs. Someone's head crashing through the living-room ceiling, mid-pogo. Kristian discovering someone had been sick on his bed. Cake on the windows. A Roman centurion proudly displaying the graze on his arm from where he'd fallen from the roof. People piling into my cabin to snort lines from a Dead or Alive record sleeve chased with tequila shots in glasses rimmed with glitter. A room of faces with sparkling silver Os around their laughing mouths.

I was on my bed, next to a bearded drag queen dressed as an enormous lobster crossed with a robot.

'Hello, I'm James,' he said. 'Whose ship is this?'

'Mine, actually.'

'Really?' He looked delighted. 'You're the Mothership?'

'I suppose I am,' I said. 'Are you a space lobster?'

'I think so.' He opened and shut his claws. 'I do feel I'm on an intergalactic adventure.'

'I'm actually the ship's computer talking to you now.'

'Mothership, where are we?'

'The end of the world, James.'

His claws made it hard for him to hold things, so I fed him cigarettes and held my glass to his lips, which were red and glittery. When we got up from the bed, my mohawk was tangled in his wig.

'We're together now,' I said.

'Onwards, Mothership.'

Outside, the sky had turned from indigo to lilac, shot with rose, and those revellers still standing, stumbled onto deck to climb the roof and wait for the world to end. Who would be damned and who saved? Those on board still in their finery, spiralling up to the heavens, or the river parting, the bowels of the Earth opening to swallow them? None of us, I reflected, would care much either way. We'd all be back-stage, drinking and gossiping, waiting for our cue to go on; partying into eternity, popping corks at the burning sky. Anyway, I'd been to Hell, more than once. Hell was a corporate Christmas party with a *Moulin Rouge* theme, or worse, *The Great Gatsby*. It was the Club's VIP before midnight, the Underground at rush hour. And Heaven? Heaven was right now . . .

Laying back on the roof's rough tar, my legs draped over the Cat's, I didn't feel the cold. James was asleep beside me, my mohawk now detached from my head and snarled in his hair. Beneath us, the sound system still blared, now only playing the first thirty seconds of every song, the deck strewn with the flotsam and jetsam of a night well spent: wigs, party streamers, broken glass, a prone body wrapped in a rug. God I was happy.

'Here it comes,' I said at the first electric streaks on the horizon and kissed the Cat, tasting the rusty tang of blood.

Above the tower blocks of Battersea and Vauxhall, the Rapture was dawning. It looked like a giant orange, rising.

Act 2

Chapter 8

'You gotta give 'em broad brushstrokes,' Gabriel Grosse was saying as I struggled to stay awake. Through my skylight dawn was breaking, my phone on loudspeaker on the pillow beside me.

I'd come to expect his calls in the small hours of the morning to impart stock phrases of directorial wisdom, accepting it as another part of the job. Because we spoke regularly, I didn't consider that I rarely saw him in person. I'd been relieved when he stopped showing up to terrorise auditions and interfere in workshops, and when he no longer came to the managers' meetings, I wasn't surprised. He may have owned the company, but the details bored him. It was only when the calls tapered off, I realised it had been weeks since I'd seen my erratic boss.

'Where's Gabriel?' I asked Archie one night, after the curtain had fallen on the second act.

He looked at me strangely. 'He's gone.'

'Gone where?'

'New York.'

'Oh. When's he back?'

Archie shrugged. 'Who knows? He hates London anyway.'

And that was how I learned Gabriel Grosse had left the building. I told myself it didn't matter he hadn't thought to let me know, it showed he trusted me with the show.

Unnerved, despite myself, at the thought of him gone completely. He'd chosen me, after all.

Now in the boardroom the managers eyed each other warily; with the boss MIA it wasn't clear who was in charge.

Hog did not attempt to hide his delight, bulldozing proceedings in an atmosphere thick with palpable loathing. The wicked part of me enjoyed watching them jostling for power. In my unique role as 'Art Department' I felt mostly immune to whatever fight was brewing, mainly because I had nothing any of them wanted.

'So *Miss* Director,' Hog turned to me. 'Who's in this week?'

Through the corner of my eye, I saw the accountant stiffen.

I sat a little straighter. 'We've got a new number with Fancy closing Act One.'

'Uh-mazing,' said Calypso.

'How d'you know it's a Closer?' said Charlie.

'Because it's Fancy,' I said and watched him roll his eyes.

Kristian was in the prop cupboard crafting a contraption from a colostomy bag.

'Look,' he said, holding it up. 'We tape it to her waist, then she can turn it on like this.'

He demonstrated, showing me the small tap that would allow it to appear as if Fancy was spontaneously pissing on stage.

'You're brilliant,' I said. 'Where d'you get the bag?'

'They sell them at the chemist.'

'I had an idea. About the piss.'

'Oh yes?'

'What about using Berocca? I reckon it'd pop under the lights.'

'I'll get some while you're in rehearsal.'

Fancy's piss-bag sorted, Kristian moved to the next task on his never-ending list. Watching him, I was filled with affection for my meticulous friend and congratulated myself for convincing the managers to hire him. Having him on the team meant we were weeks ahead on our line-ups, which put a stop to the Club's appalling practice of confirming bookings last minute and cancelling other performers if they no longer fitted the running order. Consequently, they all adored Kristian, with even Archie developing a soft spot once he'd got over his initial suspicions. And with my closest ally in the building, I was happier than I'd been for a long time. With creative free reign and a generous budget, I was busy doing what I loved and most excitingly was becoming a better director. Rich and spoiled, the Club's clientele did not equate to a generous audience, so I was learning to slaughter my darlings with a butcher's eye. *My* show would be as outrageous and shocking as anything Gabriel Grosse could conjure up, but without being exploitative. This was my most worthy philosophy. And if it was sketched only in the most general terms, I was certain of my ability to apply it when challenges arose. Until then all I wanted was to hear the crowd screaming for more, knowing part of their applause belonged to me.

Fancy shrieked when we presented her with the colostomy bag. 'You idiots,' she said. 'What's the plan?'

The plan was to gaffer-tape it to her waist, the bag hidden at the base of her back and connected to a length of clear pipe taped to her inner thigh. The new number was a reworking of her famous Prince impersonation, for which she donned a moustache and extravagantly curled quiff to perform an uncannily accurate lip-synch to *Kiss*. In recognition of Gabriel Grosse's penchant for golden shower gags we'd added an extra twist, with Fancy ripping away her purple trousers to reveal a full bush and 'pissing' into a pair of champagne glasses held by her swooning backing dancers.

For the test run, Fancy stripped down to her knickers, shoes and socks and we attached the bag Kristian had filled with water. I positioned a glass on the floor, and she took her stance with one foot either side. Screwing up her face, Fancy opened the tap on the bag, a jet of water hitting the glass with a satisfying hiss, and we fell about howling.

Fancy wiped away tears as we de-rigged her and went upstairs to change while we cleared the stage for a company rehearsal.

The dancers were lounging at the back of the auditorium, gathered round a small bundle of spines that was curled in the palm of little Sophie's hand.

'Poke him,' she cooed. 'Look, he's angry.'

'Ladies, shall we start?' I attempted a businesslike manner.

I wasn't sure when the dancers had become obsessed with collecting small animals, but lately a bull terrier puppy named 'Biggie' and a floppy-eared rabbit had been making regular appearances. Today Sophie had arrived with what looked like a miniature hedgehog in tow.

'Ladies?' I said again, louder.

Breaking up the petting zoo, the dancers reluctantly took their positions on stage. As they were trained in both classical and contemporary, the one-and-a-half-minute

Openers, which favoured hair-ography over high-kicking, posed little challenge for them.

'Music, please,' I called to the back of the room, where the lank-haired sound engineer was daydreaming behind the desk. The overture to the S&M-themed Opener came through the speakers, the dancers snapping to attention like well-trained ponies, stamping their feet and raising their riding crops above their heads.

So messed up I want you here
And in my room I want you here . . .

Out of the corner of my eye, I saw a white flash of tail disappear beneath a sofa.

'Mr Parsnip!' Gemma cried, hurrying from the stage after the errant rabbit. Sensing his opportunity, Biggie crouched down and shat extravagantly in the aisle as the rehearsal fell apart.

'What do you think about putting Sophie in the egg?' I asked Kristian on the bus back to Chelsea. 'We need to make better use of the dancers. They're bored.'

'But the egg's your signature?'

'Better than leaving it rotting on deck.'

'If you're sure.'

'We could taxi it over tomorrow morning.'

'Sounds good.'

Neither of us mentioned the Cat, who no one had seen since the party.

The Bird Lady was sitting on the bench outside the wooden gates to the mooring. That evening she was wearing a voluminous black gown, its fabric along with her face and bald head drizzled with her customary white paint. There were various theories regarding her identity. I suspected she was a former King's Road punk who'd lost her mind while retaining her sense of style. She was known to be aggressive but who could blame her? If I'd woken from my seventies dream to find myself in the Chelsea of today, I'd be pissed-off too. She glared at us as we passed, giving her a respectful berth before turning into the gate.

Felicity was on the chaise, reading a book on feminist pornography. 'Hello, bunnies,' she smiled as we came in.

'Hey, sweet,' I said, flopping down beside her, Kristian collapsing in the armchair next to the heater.

'You both look like you've escaped from the asylum.'

'What gave us away?'

'The muscle twitching under Kristian's left eye.'

It was true neither of us were looking our best; shadows beneath my bloodshot eyes, Kristian's face hollow from his long hours in the prop cupboard.

'I've still got to mix fresh blood for tonight,' he was mumbling now.

'Do you think I could teach the dancers fire?' I wondered out loud.

'The Co-op might have beetroot juice.'

'I'd have to check the Club's insurance . . . Might be optimistic.'

There was a huffing sound as Felicity left the room, taking her book with her. I knew Kristian and I were becoming intolerable and that Felicity was feeling left out. From her point of view it must have seemed the easiest thing in the world to create a number for her, but the Club had rigid rules regarding the female bodies allowed on stage, with curves strictly forbidden unless an orifice took the starring role, and

I was reluctant to explain that her body type was considered undesirable, or suggest a penetration stunt about which I had mixed feelings in the context of the Club. I had no issue if a performer arrived with it already in their repertoire, but attempting it to secure a booking was something else entirely.

Kristian appeared to be falling asleep, so I went downstairs to make it up to Felicity, but she'd shut herself in her cabin.

'Do you want a cup of tea?' I said, knocking softly on the door.

'No, thank you,' came a clipped voice from inside.

Lacking the energy to cajole, I went to my own cabin to pass out for a couple of hours before returning to Soho. I crawled into bed in my clothes, kicking my shoes to the floor, inhaling the pillow's familiar smell of hairspray, cigarettes and perfume.

From down the corridor, I heard the front door open and a few moments later the pad of soft footsteps in the corridor.

The door creaked open, and the Cat's wary face peered around the door frame. 'Awright.' He slunk cautiously into the room.

I took in his appearance with distaste; his hair was full of plaster dust, giving it a greyish hue.

'What happened to you?' I said.

He grinned. 'I was, uh, helping a friend.'

'Well you're not getting into bed like that.'

'Shall I have a bath?'

'I think you'd better.'

I scowled after him as he closed the door softly, irritated by his meekness. A few moments later, I heard the water running and my irritation turned to anger. Why should he assume that he could show up for food and sex any time he wanted? I got out of bed.

In the bathroom, the Cat was already sitting in the half-full tub with both taps running.

Ignoring the loveliness of him in the water, I said, 'Actually, I'd rather be alone this evening.'

He looked up with the eyes of a stray who has never been sure of their invitation to stay. 'Okay.'

'You can have a bath but I need to sleep. I'm at the Club tonight.'

'I can drive you.'

For a moment, laziness almost won out. 'I'll take the bus.' I turned to go.

'You're embarrassed.'

I stopped, wondering if I'd heard correctly. He'd said it so quietly.

'Pardon?'

'You don't want to be seen with me.'

'That isn't true,' I said. 'But it's work.'

'Sure.'

'You're not being nice,' I said, stung by the new dismissive tone in his voice. 'And I'm not having this conversation while you're in the bloody bath.'

'Kitty,' the Cat shook his head. 'Who calls their boyfriend that?'

I narrowed my eyes. 'You're not my boyfriend,' I said, and went back down the corridor, pulling my cabin door closed with a bang. I was furious, but not with him. The Cat's accusations, though skewed through the prism of his pain, were true.

'I'm *over* people being angry with me,' I complained, pushing my head beneath the pillow.

Not long after I heard the Cat leaving. He didn't slam the door. It wasn't his way.

The following morning, Kristian and I hoisted the egg down the pontoons and into a waiting minicab. At the Club, we carried it through the main entrance and deposited it on stage, where it stood looking scruffier than ever.

'Am I going to look stupid?' Sophie seemed unconvinced.

'Don't worry, I've done this before.'

'I'll feel silly.'

'Trust me?'

My dance vocabulary was limited, but I knew if I could get her to start thinking like a choreographer, I could shape her suggestions into a number. I explained how I saw it working and we began the process of interpreting words into movement. Step by step, gesture by gesture, the dance started to appear. After an hour, we were both getting excited. The music was Sophie's suggestion, a remix of one of the previous summer's hits. The track began with a vocal of quavering sweetness over echoing underwater sounds, before exploding into a spiralling drop of crunching electronic beats.

'How high can you jump?' I said.

'Jump?'

I attempted to show her what I meant.

Sophie looked at the stage, which was not particularly wide, and took a couple of steps back until she was standing against the proscenium arch. Gathering her strength, she sprang forwards, her legs scissoring into perfect splits.

I whooped with delight. 'That's it, that's the drop!'

'Hey.'

I turned to see Lila watching from the doorway.

'Whatcha doing?' she said.

'Just working on a new number.'

'Oh. I didn't know about that.' Lila looked at Sophie who was suddenly absorbed fiddling with her bracelet. 'Where'd that egg come from?'

'It's mine,' I said.

Lila smiled. 'It looks kind of wonky.'

'We're going to fix it up before the show.'

'Uh-huh.'

I could see she was unhappy, but Lila had plum roles in countless numbers, it wouldn't hurt her to share the spotlight for once.

When she'd gone Sophie let out a wail. 'Ruby, she's going to be so *pissed* at me.'

'Really?'

'*Yes.*'

'Well, she'll just have to get over it.'

'She said it was wonky.'

'It's going to be amazing.' I laughed. 'Come on, let's go from the top.'

I left the Club in a happy mood and walked through the backstreets to Carnaby Street. No longer anxious every time I used my bank card, my spending habits had caught up accordingly.

The first time I'd received my pay cheque I'd marched upstairs to the office. 'Where's the rest?' I demanded. 'I should be getting twice that.'

The accountant looked at me curiously. 'Tax?' he said.

I'd back-pedalled but it was too late, he'd already caught a glimpse of my history of cash-in-hand employment and ignorance of the adult world. Well, never mind. Even after tax the money was more than I'd hoped for.

Liberty was my favourite place to express my new-found sense of solvency, drifting among the make-up counters, running my fingers over silk scarves and glossy bags in the warmth of its mock-Tudor halls. That evening I spent a week's worth of mooring fees on a dress that was slippery and orange. It was essential, I felt, to have an arsenal of appropriate day-to-night wear.

I wandered back towards Shaftesbury Avenue, enjoying the purple shopping bag swinging from my wrist, with the feeling I belonged. For a long time, I'd been estranged from new London that had sprung up with such alarming speed, swathes of streets demolished to make way for bigger and better transport links to bring the people in. And though it hurt to see it overcome, lately I'd developed a new perspective. Perhaps every generation was destined to mourn the Soho of the time before? Nights of tumbling through doorways into secret piano bars and speakeasies; the louche members' clubs where YBAs and rock stars rubbed shoulders with bar-stool philosophers. But even those halcyon days were dreaming of a more distant past, when rent boys spoke in coded Polari and aristocrats pissed themselves where they sat. Once, I'd overheard two well-dressed men walking into the Groucho. 'So where was Francis Bacon's place then?' one of them asked the other. 'There.' His companion gestured confidently to a Caffè Nero on the corner where no members' club had ever been. Everyone had their own myth of Soho and beyond a certain point nostalgia was never a good look. The city was changing – had been changing for years – and I was discovering what it might now become. Something sleek, rich and clean.

Sophie would make her debut after the first Opener from which she was exempt. Her costume was a flesh-coloured bodystocking embroidered with white feathers and a matching cap, feathered sprays at her wrists and ankles. She looked beautiful and fragile as she fussed with her cap, scraps of down drifting to the dressing-room floor.

'I'm nervous!' she cried, hopping up and down, flexing her pointe shoes.

'Nerves are *good*.' I gave her a hug, feeling the tiny bones through the skin of her back.

I went downstairs to the side of the stage and laid a hand over my fluttering heart. I was nervous too.

Lila appeared beside me, a black kimono over her costume, as the track's dreamy beginning drifted over the speakers, the curtains opening to reveal the egg bathed in delicate pink and blue light. Kristian and Archie had done an excellent job bringing it back to life, the surface glittering with pearly iridescence beneath the follow-spot's beam.

The door on the egg flew open as the first beat dropped. Two delicate hands, fingers hooked into claws, reached out towards the audience. They were followed by a pair of slender legs and finally, Sophie's lovely face.

Crumpling elegantly to the floor, she got to her feet and took a couple of stumbling steps, that were half-ballet, half-Bambi, her arms cricked and awkward.

I looked at the audience. They weren't applauding, but they weren't talking either.

On stage, Sophie's crippled moves were becoming more athletic, gathering speed, the gestures of her arms expanding, growing wider, and I could feel the energy of the crowd start to rise.

Beside me, I could see the whites of Lila's eyes as Sophie dropped to the floor, dragging herself forward on her elbows before flipping backwards in a gymnastic twist. Then she was on her feet again as the track built with an urgent staccato beat, tottering backwards on her toes until she was almost against the proscenium arch, ready for the leap.

Her eyes locked on her mark. If she landed wrong, she'd be off the side of the stage. In the moments before the drop, the track fell away in a suspended break of shimmering silence. A sensation between nausea and excitement rose behind my lips and I fought the urge to close my eyes.

The track dropped, and Sophie flew up, up, in a perfect gazelle-leap across the stage. By the time she landed, the audience was howling as the strobe kicked in, the dance exploding in a crescendo of spins that were pure physical joy. There was a movement at my shoulder, and I saw that Lila was gone.

I found Sophie in the wings, the crowd still baying their approval out front. We looked at each other, screamed, and embraced. She was slick with sweat and trembling with adrenalin.

'How did that feel?' I laughed.

'Was it good?'

'Can't you hear them?'

She gave a squeal that made me glow with pleasure.

After she'd towelled herself down and reapplied her make-up, Sophie broke Club-protocol by going out into the crowd still wearing her costume and was immediately mobbed by fans.

I watched her disappear into the party. That heady moment when you were the girl everyone wanted to know.

Did I miss it? I checked myself. Inside me, the little showgirl was buzzing as if I'd folded part of her into Sophie and soared with her into the light. And somewhere deeper, an echo sad and sweet, of something passing by.

Chapter 9

I'd remained long after the Club closed, partying with the rest of the dregs not yet ready to face the night's end. Enzo had tied a napkin over his eyes and dropped his jeans to mix me a drink blindfold. There were lines of bad cocaine behind the lighting desk with Reg. It was Wednesday night, then Thursday morning.

At 10 a.m. I was woken by a call from my grand-mother, my eyes struggling to focus on her initials on the screen.

'GJ,' I croaked.

'Darling, have you just woken up?'

'More or less . . .'

'It's ten o'clock.'

'Yes, I know,' I said, unable to keep the annoyance out of my voice.

Her tone changed to one of anger. 'Well, darling, I have no time for *layabouts*.'

'I work at a nightclub . . .' I started to say, but goddamn it, if she hadn't hung up on me.

I collapsed back on to the pillow. 'For fucksake . . .'

Lately, the calls had been getting worse, adding to the maelstrom of communication from the Club that was now part of my life. I wasn't always able to pick up, but this was the first time I'd exposed her to my frustration.

Too upset to fall back asleep, I slumped out of bed, one hand reaching to steady myself against the rocking of the boat, until I realised it was me.

Another Soho morning, another zombie in the crowd as I weaved my way to work. Approaching the Club, I didn't see the wall-sized man outside the stage door until he blocked my path with one enormous arm.

'No,' he said in a thick Russian accent.

I squinted up at him. 'I work here.'

He was well over six feet tall, dressed entirely in black, with a ponderous head that looked hewn from marble.

'No one coming in.'

A stab of rage signalling the arrival of my hangover proper. 'I have a rehearsal at three, so I'm afraid I have to come in.'

He looked back impassively. I folded my arms. Neither of us moved.

'Look, is there someone you can call?' I said.

He peered down as if deciding whether to hurl me from the doorstep, then he muttered into his radio. While he waited for a response, I checked my phone and saw I'd missed several calls from Kristian. The radio crackled, followed by a low burst of Russian as someone on the other end replied.

'Who you are?' he asked.

'I'm the director.'

He muttered again, listening to the reply when it came, and stood back to let me pass.

'Thank you,' I said, squeezing sideways around his bulk.

In the main room, a dozen black-clad giants were standing guard on every doorway and in front of the bar. Three of them were pacing the stage like the world's most lumbering chorus line, wearing expressions that were a curious mix of tough guy and vaguely sheepish.

Archie was perched on a sofa watching the spectacle unfold.

'Archie, what's happening?' I said.

'Hog's taken over the Club.'

'What?'

'I know.' He was grinning. 'Mad.'

The dancers started to arrive. They stood in a huddle, stealing skittish looks at the guards, who in turn eyed the dancers' menagerie of small animals adding to the general confusion in the room.

'*Baaabe*,' said Sophie. 'What's going on?'

'Some sort of dick-swinging contest,' I said grumpily. 'Just ignore them and let's get on with the rehearsal.'

Retrieving the mic from the sound desk, I walked to the middle of the room. 'Excuse me,' my voice boomed over the speakers. 'But we need to clear the stage.'

All faces turned towards the new source of noise.

'The stage,' I gestured with a sweeping motion.

The guards standing beneath the proscenium arch looked down as if discovering their feet for the first time and shuffled off looking chastened.

I cued the music as the dancers took their places and a sleazy reworking of the Iggy Pop classic began to play.

Now I wanna be your dog . . .

Kristian was waiting for me in the prop cupboard. We looked at each other and burst out laughing.

'Can you believe this?' I said.

'I couldn't get in this morning. I was stuck outside for twenty minutes.'

'They wouldn't let me in either.'

'They're all insane.'

I sat down in a chair. 'What do we do?'

'Carry on?'

'I guess so.'

Archie stuck his head around the door. 'Ruby, Hog wants to see you.'

'When?'

'Now. In Gabriel's office.'

'Shit,' I said. Then, 'Gabriel has an office?'

Climbing the stairs to the topmost floor above the main office, a place I'd never been, I tried to prepare for whatever was about to happen. What could he possibly want from me?

At the top was a tiny landing and a single closed door. 'Come in,' a voice barked when I knocked.

The office was poky, empty but for a desk, a clothes rail and a couple of chairs. Nothing on the walls.

Hog was behind the desk, which looked too small for him, like primary school furniture.

'Siddown.' He gestured to a chair in front.

Cautiously, I took a seat.

He looked at me for a long moment. 'I've got a new name for that number with the Chinese girl.'

'Oh . . .?'

'There's a Nasty Nip in the Air.' He guffawed at his own joke.

It took me a beat to realise he was referring to Fancy's Hair Hang.

'She's Korean-American,' I said.

'Same difference.'

I didn't reply, retreating to the quiet, still place I kept in reserve for times of trouble.

'There's gonna be some changes round here,' he said, his small eyes gleaming. 'I wanna see proper women, with proper tits.'

I blinked.

'Glamour. No more freaks. No more anorexic little girls.'

He looked at me for a long moment as if deciding whether I was up to the task, and I found myself wondering how often he had to bleach his hair to maintain that shade of Monroe-blond. I understood the sane emotional response ought to be alarm but it was too absurd, Hog as unconvincing as Gabriel Grosse in his impresario mode. It was all facade, concealing a wavering masculinity, uncertain of itself and how to be.

'We'll talk,' Hog said, my creative briefing over. 'Send Archie up, will you?'

That afternoon, the managers shut themselves in their office, strained silence emanating from behind the door. Occasionally you'd see one of them hurry past looking agitated, but no one came to tell us what was happening.

Holed-up in the prop cupboard with Kristian and Archie, I refreshed my emails for the thirteenth time that day. 'Still nothing,' I said. 'I'm going for a look.'

Enzo was restocking the main bar, looking grumpier than usual.

'Smoke?' I said, miming the gesture for the benefit of the guards nearby.

He nodded, and we left the room, staying silent until we stepped through a hidden door halfway down the main staircase, to the room where the surveillance monitors were kept. We lit up and stood side by side watching the slow movements of Hog's taskforce on the small black-and-white screens.

'Dark times, Madame,' Enzo said.

'It's ridiculous.'

'In my opinion, it serves the Americans right for being the worst kind of scumbags.'

'Hog's just as bad.'

'Ah, but at least he's stupid.'

'Gabriel Grosse isn't stupid?'

'Unfortunately, he's just an arsehole.'

I looked at him, handsome and surly under the overhead strip light. The surveillance room felt suddenly very small.

Enzo stubbed his cigarette out on the wall. 'Madame. Regretfully, I must leave you and get back to my grunt work.'

He opened the door, and we stepped out in a billow of smoke.

That night, Hog sat at the front on one of the VIP tables, with a group of hatchet-faced men I hadn't seen before, champagne on ice, and a clutch of women with augmented faces and rubbery-looking chests. Lila was there too, wearing a red bandage-dress, laughing at something Hog had said.

'Why doesn't he just cock his leg and piss all over the VIP seats?' I said to Kristian.

'I'm pretty sure someone's already done that.'

The curtains closed on Sophie's dance to a roar of applause and Hog beckoned me over with two fingers.

I had to bend to hear what he was saying, his breath blasting my face. 'No. More. Skinny. Little. Girls.'

'The audience love her.'

'Get rid.'

I nodded once, then returned to where Kristian was standing. 'Can we go home now?'

'If they'll let us.'

The giant man was still at the stage door when we stepped out into the street.

'Goodnight,' I said.

'Goodnight.' He sounded almost shy.

Maciek was still awake when we got home. He'd shaved off his eyebrows the previous week, dyeing the rest of his hair silver, and resembled a shimmering alien perched at the kitchen counter, eating Japanese nattō with chopsticks.

'You're eating solids,' I said.

'Nattō isn't food.' He sounded weary. 'It's healthy.'

'Well, the Club's been taken over by the Russians.'

'*Amazing*.'

'Not really.'

'I like your life,' he said, studying a gooey strand of fermented soya beans.

'You can have it for a while.'

'Mine too,' said Kristian. 'I'm going to bed.' He went to his cabin, and we heard the door slide shut. I envied him in that moment, unaffected by what was happening while I was danced like a puppet on a string. But he'd always been better than me at staying out of trouble.

Lying in my cabin I couldn't sleep, trying to imagine the scene when Gabriel Grosse learned what Hog had done. It was both hilarious and awful. What would happen now? Hog wasn't playing, Gabriel Grosse just a rich boy, but I couldn't imagine him giving up without a fight. On impulse

I dialled his number, knowing he wouldn't answer, and listened to it ring out in the dark.

'Morning,' I said to the giant at the door. 'We need to come in.'

He reached for his radio.

'You must get bored standing out here all day,' I said.

'No.'

I smiled. 'What's your name?'

'Dmitry. You can go,' he gestured.

'Bye, Dmitry.'

'Goodbye.'

'That went well,' said Kristian as we made our way upstairs.

'I'll break him.'

Lila was in the prop cupboard with Archie. It was unusual to see her in the Club before lunch.

'Did something happen?' I said.

'We're just going through the line-up,' said Lila. 'Hog's kind of concerned.'

'Yes, real women. He told me.'

'He asked if I could help.'

There was a pause while I interpreted the meaning behind her words.

'Fresh ideas,' said Lila. 'More sexy, y'know?'

'Right.'

'The show's been kind of freaky lately.'

I ignored the barb. 'Well, let me know when you're ready and we'll schedule a workshop.'

For a moment her face hardened. It was imperceptible, but it was enough.

I turned to Archie. 'Sophie's out for the time being, so we'll need a replacement.'

'Okay,' he said, scrambling for his iPad.

'Thanks for coming,' I said to Lila. 'It's appreciated.'

After she'd gone, no one spoke, Archie's fingers tip-tapping on the keys the only sound.

Two days passed with no word from Gabriel Grosse or the managers, who'd apparently decided the best way of dealing with the situation was to pretend it wasn't happening, as they each took their turn to pay lip-service at the squatted office on the top floor.

In the prop cupboard, Kristian and I were engaged in our own form of collaboration, scouring the websites of several London-based escort agencies.

'I can't believe we're doing this,' said Kristian. 'This has nothing to do with theatre.'

'You could say that sex was the ultimate performance.'

'There's no way we can afford it.'

'What about the fetish forums? There must be some exhibitionists who'd do it for free.'

'Two women?'

'Trickier, for sure.'

We'd been working on Hog's latest request without success; staging a live-sex show was proving more challenging than either of us had anticipated.

'Coffee,' I announced. 'I'm buying. Do we need cake?'

Taking the shortcut via the stage, I heard voices coming from below. On a sofa in the main room, Lila was talking to a pair of fire performers with whom I had a workshop scheduled the following day.

She looked up at the sound of my footsteps, panic on her face and I understood I'd walked in on a hijacking.

Crossing the room to where they were sitting, I tried to

keep my expression neutral. 'Glad you could come in early. Thanks for getting things started,' I said to Lila.

The look that passed across her features put me in mind of a snake about to strike, then she rearranged them into a smile. 'Sure thing.'

My eyes followed as she left the room. She didn't look back – she didn't have to. Gabriel Grosse wasn't the only one with a power-grab on his hands.

After the workshop I left the Club, stepping past the giant on the doorstep onto the street. I needed to walk and to think.

It was quiet in Golden Square that afternoon, with only a handful of office workers eating lunch al fresco, the farthest possible distance from the ragged man shouting into the branches of a horse chestnut tree, at something only he could see. I chose a bench nearby, comforted by his obvious craziness.

I closed my eyes, trying to see my way through this new conundrum. That the managers wouldn't support me, I knew. I was still the new girl and an unknown quantity. That left only Hog, and Lila was far better equipped in knowing how to handle him.

The man who'd been shouting fell to his knees and began to laugh, his face full of light turned towards the sky. Watching him, I found myself pondering how would it be, to be free of all this scrabbling? With the lights on, the Club was just another dirty building in Soho – it was a sparkler in a bottle, a con. I imagined myself quitting, Archie's smirk as if he'd known all along and Lila stepping into my shoes. Hauling the egg from the Club and putting it to work amidst cabaret gossip. Scraping by once more. Fuck all of them, I thought. I'm going nowhere.

By the end of the week, Hog was still in charge, the Russian giants as familiar as the cleaners who came to mop the previous night's fluids. In rehearsals, Lila embraced her new role as Nemesis with the same commitment she did any other. If I called for the lights to be red, she would demand green, leaving the stage to harangue Reg at the lighting desk, with the dancers looking on. Line-ups were changed behind my back – Archie hedging his bets – and, growing bolder, she began showing up during workshops, forcing me into a gruesome pantomime of trying to get rid of her without the performers realising. No use speaking to the managers, they were too busy scrambling to find their own place in the new upside-down order, all of us waiting to see where we'd land. Too stressed out to sleep, my eyes, always sensitive, now fluttered uncontrollably on entering the Club, and I wondered what was wrong with me, that it was Lila I thought of as I dragged myself from bed, heavy with dread at the prospect of another day, and not the fact I was going to work in a war zone. But things had become normal very quickly.

A fortnight into the new regime I received another summons to Hog's office on the topmost floor, after the curtain had fallen on Saturday night. I found him tucking into an oozing burger, ketchup and grease mingling with the smell of perspiration in the room.

I stood in front of his desk, having declined his offer to sit. 'We need more time,' I said.

'Some don't think so.'

'They might find it more difficult in practice.'

'Hmm.' Hog chewed thoughtfully.

My gaze strayed to the clock on the wall: 4.47 a.m. What was I doing here? I felt vaguely delirious, dangerously close to telling Hog what I thought of his half-baked hardman routine, but instead heard myself promising that, yes, it could be done. Somehow, we'd make it happen.

'You've got a week,' he said, before I was dismissed.

I left the office and went to get my coat from the prop cupboard, feeling like the worst kind of creep. I'd spent a lifetime avoiding situations that required a *Yes*, when what you meant was *Go fuck yourself*, but I was not prepared to let go of the Club. Not like this, not yet.

Chapter 10

'Ready?' Kristian was waiting at the front door in a grey wool coat, its collar turned up around his pale face. Outside, Monday morning, muggy and grey.

The worst thing about having a job and working for other people, I reflected, was you couldn't *not go*. You were a moving part, a cog in the machine. Even if the place you worked was a madhouse.

'I feel sick,' I said.

'We're going to be late.'

We sat on the bus in silence, my anxiety climbing as we crossed the invisible border into Soho, *I don't want to go*, running like a mantra through my head.

When we arrived at the stage door, the giant was not on his doorstep. I stepped forward and punched in the door code. Nothing happened.

'Archie's texted,' said Kristian, looking at his phone. He tried the new digits and the door clicked open.

In the upstairs corridor, a figure was standing at the foot of the stairs. They turned towards the sound of our footsteps. The OM gave a curt nod and disappeared upstairs.

Kristian and I exchanged a glance, then hurried to the prop cupboard where we found Archie alone.

'Did Gabriel come back?' I said, breathless.

Archie shook his head. 'No, just the OM.'

'What about Hog?'

'He's gone.'

'Gone where?'

'Just gone.'

An email arrived informing us that the managers' meeting would be going ahead.

'We'd better go up,' said Archie.

'What the actual fuck is going on?' I said.

In the boardroom, the OM was sitting grim-faced at the head of the long table. The managers on either side looked nervous and I wondered how far they'd gone in transferring their loyalty to Gabriel Grosse's usurper.

The OM began to speak, projected figures for the week rolling out with no mention of the Russian takeover. I waited for the moment when someone would interrupt demanding an explanation, but nobody did.

The meeting ended, and the OM gestured I should stay behind. He remained silent until the last of the managers had gone. There was a sucking sound as the door closed, sealing us inside.

'So,' he said. 'The show.'

I thought: *The fucking show.*

'We need a new approach. As you are aware we're a business foremost. And with any business each department must be held to the same enumerative accountability.'

'Right . . .' I tried to locate myself on the same page.

'Quotas,' he said. 'Targets. We need a system,' he continued. 'Optimum hours for working on auditions and new numbers, measured against the success of each, in terms of audience feedback, bar-spend, etcetera.'

'With respect,' I said, 'I'm not sure you can quantify theatre that way.'

His lips tightened. 'Understand, I expect you to be stringent.'

I recalled the company's habit of implementing impossible incentives that were quickly forgotten.

'Could you email me an example of the system you'd like us to use?' I said, knowing nothing would be sent. 'I'm not familiar with business models.'

He looked at me coldly and I knew I'd made an enemy. 'Of course, honey,' he said. 'And I look forward to reports of your progress.'

Overnight, the Club returned to the former status quo as if Hog had never been. His reign had lasted barely a fortnight. Kristian was given the job of clearing his possessions from the office and I'd joined him in the task. Inside, we found a selection of police and military uniforms, size XXL, and a bullet-proof vest, which we smuggled back to the boat and sold quietly on eBay. Between us, we agreed a pay-off as the most likely explanation for Hog's disappearance, though sometimes I entertained a fantasy of him, feet encased in concrete, floating at the bottom of the Thames. Perhaps not far from the boat.

I resumed my routine of auditions, workshops and rehearsals, but something had been lost. It was the same ennui I recognised in other members of staff, a kind of weary bitterness that encouraged lassitude in some and dishonesty in others. If before I'd given my all, now I'd give just enough. My pride was bruised and I was angry; at Gabriel Grosse for abandoning me, at the managers for their cowardice. At Lila. She'd rejoined the dancers in their dressing room without a fuss, but it was she who affected me most. Now I found myself searching for the agenda behind every smile, and after a while I could see people searching back.

Whether all this had a part in what was happening to my eyes, I couldn't be sure. Hours spent staring at the stage lights didn't help. My eyelids, which had always fluttered in times of tiredness and extreme emotion, now did it constantly. It should have been a red flag but I'd never been good at gauging my own limits. And in the predatory ecosystem of the Club, my lack of poker-face seemed a fatal disadvantage.

The Botox clinic was a five-minute walk from the Club. The walls were decorated with magenta-and-gold flocked wall-paper, the front desk manned by two mannequins with perfectly smooth and shining foreheads.

'Could you show me the areas of concern?' the Botox doctor said. He'd already asked my age, studying my face for flaws in a way that made me squirm.

'It's not wrinkles I'm worried about,' I said. 'I need something to stop me blinking.'

I pointed to my eyes, which were sore to the point of weeping.

'I see.'

'Will it help?'

'It should do, yes.'

Lying on the white table, I heard as much as felt the pricks administered in a circle around my eye sockets. The procedure took less than twenty minutes and when it was over, I paid on my card and went back to the Club.

For the rest of the afternoon and all the following day, I kept checking on the progress as the toxin took effect. By day two, my blinking had slowed and the area around my eyes was strangely immobile.

'Kristian, look,' I said. 'Can you see the difference?'

He looked at me. 'What have you done?'

'I got my eyes fixed. Look, I can't move them.'

I smiled at him, watching myself in the mirror. Sure enough, even with the corners of my mouth stretched into a joker's grin, my eyes remained the same.

'I'm not sure I like it,' said Kristian.

'It's just for now,' I said. 'While I'm broken.'

Summer announced itself with a slow turning up of heat, pollen mingling with the petrol fumes, making people irritable and sneezy. On the Underground, pre-recorded messages broadcast warnings about the dangers of dehydration, Londoners vibrating with hostility in the rammed carriages, chattering tourists oblivious to the barely suppressed violence in their midst.

Below street level, I was dimly aware of the changing season. Once or twice, Archie, Kristian and I attempted our meetings up on the Beach, but it made us uncomfortable, and we went back down again. Daylight was for lightweights and summer for those with nothing better to do.

Then I began to notice the godlike men roaming the streets, which alerted me to the arrival of the Olympics in London. I'd been aware of it only dimly, lurking at the edge of my reality, like war in a faraway country. But now I saw the city gripped by a patriotic fervour I did not understand.

The Opening Ceremony would coincide with Rose's next visit, and frankly the Olympics was asking for it. I emailed Rose to discuss the homage we'd stage the same night the real event would be broadcast across the world. Since her visit we'd developed a correspondence, her poetic musings arriving in my inbox at odd times of day and night, which I kept in a special file to look over later.

Dear Ruby. Spring equinox today, the winds of change in the air in dirty old New York City . . .

Ruby. There's something grand and awful I'm working on here. Could do with your keen eye.

On the day she arrived, I found her sitting with Athena on one of the sofas by the stage.

'See you later, Rosie-baby,' Athena said, throwing me a wink that made heat rise to my cheeks, for I was harbouring a schoolgirl-crush on the charismatic MC.

Rose and I embraced. 'How are you, stranger?' she said.

'I honestly don't know.'

She laughed gently. 'Oh, I heard a few things.'

'Probably all true.'

'This place attracts crazy. You get used to it.'

At that moment Lila wandered in with Charlie, and had we been cats we would have hissed. Charlie came over to say hello to Rose and when they'd gone, she was quiet.

'You know, I've known that kid a long time,' Rose said. 'I understand her behaviour might not always make sense.'

'She's a nightmare.'

'Some might call her a product of her environment. You could show her a different way.'

'I'm not sure the moral high-ground carries much weight around here.'

Rose smiled. 'Perhaps not. But it's worth knowing which way North is. Especially in the dark.'

'Hmm,' I replied, but knew she was right. Lila, an exceptional dancer, had given her best years to the Club, with its promise of a shortcut to stardom; when any night could be the one a famous director might spot you from the crowd. But the men who came to party were not looking for undiscovered talent. And now the show was all she had.

A week before the Opening Ceremony, I was sweating out a hangover in the prop cupboard when my phone rang, an unfamiliar number on the screen. Usually, I'd send unknowns straight to voicemail, but for some reason this time I answered.

'Hello?'

'Babe?'

I froze.

'Magda?'

'My *krásná*! *Milacik!*'

My head was spinning. Seven years since I'd heard that voice. She sounded far away.

'Hold on, I'm just taking this outside.'

I took the phone up to the Beach where I took a breath before saying again, 'Magda?'

'Babe, it's my birthday!'

'It's your birthday today?'

'Yes!'

I laughed. 'Well happy birthday.'

'I miss you; I want to see you.'

'I've missed you too.'

'Come and see me, babe, I've got a boat.'

'A what?'

She cackled, coughed. 'A boat, a big boat! It's at my place. We'll take it on the canal.'

The conversation was already taking a turn for the surreal.

'Will you come?'

'Of course I will.'

After I hung up, I stared at my phone for a long time, lost in thought. Magda. Was it possible things were better?

From where I was standing on the roof of the Club, I was less than ten minutes' walk from the place I'd first seen her. I was twenty, Magda a few years and several lifetimes older, holding court in an underground cave that served as the cloakroom at a legendary Ska night on Wardour Street. A mop of dyed black hair dusted at the sides with peroxide blond, platform boots, pinstripes and braces. Slanted blue eyes that almost disappeared with the breadth of her smile. She was surrounded by grizzled men in sharp suits and fedora hats, who were hanging on her every word, dazzled by her light. The brightest thing I'd seen.

In the apartment opposite the roof, two men were engaged in a bout of athletic afternoon sex. Watching their bodies colliding somewhere between lust and violence, a cold feeling spread through me. Hadn't we always celebrated Magda's birthday in November? I realised with a queasy jolt, that it was July.

The day of the Opening Ceremony arrived, with events organised all over the city. In the hours before, taken by an overwhelming curiosity, I found myself wrapping up rehearsals early and hurrying to the sweltering Underground.

The screening party was at a working men's club off Bethnal Green Road, a popular cabaret venue where I'd performed countless times. Inside the shabby hall, a large screen had been rigged onstage in front of a gold tinsel curtain. Several performers of my acquaintance were there, and the lanky drummer from a band I'd sung with for a while. Friendly people, stylish in their cheap clothes, and I felt shy seeing them in this familiar stomping ground where not so long ago we'd shared a dressing room, gossiping over plastic cups of bubbly wine. I felt different now, one foot in another world, uncertain of where I belonged.

We stood waiting, holding onto our drinks, others deciding to sit on the swirly red and brown carpet, stickier even than the Club's. Finally, the screen flickered to life. The internet connection was poor and at first it seemed we'd miss the start, but then it stabilised, and an ironic cheer went up as the picture came into view – because what could be more camp than an Opening Ceremony viewing party? The cheers quickly died down as people began to watch.

An hour later, I emerged into the dying light, my head full of images of great brick towers shooting from the green earth, Mary Poppins aerialists floating from the sky on umbrellas, NHS nurses pushing glowing perambulators. Glorious. I'd stayed until the last possible minute, unable to tear myself away.

Watching it unfold, I'd felt a terrible lack, of being on the outside of something. Of having always been on the outside. And as the excitement in the room continued to build, for the first time in my life I'd ached to be part of the crowd.

Through the warm June evening I carried my new sense of shame, back to Soho and the kingdom beneath the street, where that night we'd stage our own ceremony of cardboard and glue we'd put together in the dark.

The follow-spot swept across the rippling curtains, the lights flashing on and off, as the Mad Hatter, no longer hatted in shorts and a sweatband, came jogging through the crowd. This was Ned, an actor and the Club's resident 'little person', who had a side-hustle manning the door at M&M's World on Leicester Square. In his hand he held the Olympic torch ablaze with several sparklers.

The curtains opened to reveal a stepped podium where the dancers, in unflattering eighties Lycra, stood ready to receive their medals. A huge cheer went up when Rose, representing Russia in gold hot pants, stepped into the spotlight, her arms raised in victory.

The dancers dismounted the podium as the torchbearer reached the stage, handing it to Sophie as Rose removed the golden hot pants. Naked from the waist down, she turned her back to the audience and sized up the stage, pivoting forward into a solid handstand, the dancers at either side catching her legs to hold her in place.

Then, wincing only slightly, Sophie lifted the torch high before lowering it down, down into the Bermuda Triangle of Rose's arsehole. The crowd as they say, went wild, and I raised a tired but patriotic smile.

Chapter 11

August in London. In night-life terms, a month best forgotten, the Club emptier than usual with a sluggish crowd, bulked out with the sort of punter who normally didn't make the cut. Men in tight shirts over swollen pecs, girls with bottled tans and stripes in their hair. Life backstage was equally slow, with no private parties or corporate events we plugged away at the show, though sometimes being underground on a sweltering afternoon felt like penance. There was no word from Gabriel Grosse; it was as if he'd disappeared completely.

Kristian and I were in the main room, putting the finishing touches to a 'Notting Hill Carnival' decor scheme of plastic palm fronds and tropical flowers that looked wrong against the Club's interior.

'Where's this dancer?' I grumbled, itching to get home.

My phone buzzed with a message.

I think Im here? Whers the door?

'I'll try and find him,' I said to Kristian. 'You go. I'll see you onboard.'

There was no one outside the stage door. I looked both ways then walked around the corner to the alley. There, in the neon glow of the adjacent sex shop, was a boy. He was looking at me with one eyebrow raised and did not look sorry at all.

'That for me?' he said.

I looked down and saw I was still holding a bouquet of tropical flowers.

'You're late.' I pointed it at him.

'Do you know how to get in? I'm meeting the director.'

'That's me.'

'Really?'

I was used to people double-checking this curious fact. 'Really,' I said.

He smiled, showing a row of perfect white teeth. 'Been looking forward to meeting you.'

Sitting on the stage, I listened to the boy with growing amusement. He hadn't stopped talking since I'd fished him from the alley, or made any move to show me his audition piece. He was shockingly good-looking, with skin the colour of milky tea and a tangle of gravity-defying black curls springing from the front of a black pork-pie hat. A pencil moustache, grown to make him look older, I guessed.

'I'm an artist,' he said. 'And an art director and a choreographer. I'd like to choreograph something for you here.'

I tried to picture Lila's reaction. It was almost worth suggesting.

He looked around the Club. 'It's a nice place,' he said. 'Very *os-ten-tac-ious*.'

It was my turn to raise an eyebrow.

'No, thank *you*,' he said, when our strange interview was over. He hadn't danced a step and I'd forgotten to ask.

I took him as far as the stage door, then went to fetch my coat from the prop cupboard. When I stepped out onto the street, he was waiting for me there.

'Hello again,' I said.

'Headed to the station?' he said, not missing a beat.

'Shaftesbury Avenue.'

'Walk and talk?'

There was more he wanted to tell me. Concepts for shows, his long arms painting pictures in the air, dodging round lamp posts like a Soho remake of *Singin' in the Rain*. Aware I was being hustled, I didn't hold it against him. There were a lot of dancers in London and talent alone would only get you so far.

'Come for a drink?' he said when we reached the border of Chinatown.

I weighed up my options. If I headed home now, I might actually get some sleep.

'It'll be free,' he added.

Fine, I thought. *Let's play.*

He took me to a tacky club off Piccadilly where he worked as a promoter. These were young, good-looking club rats, employed to bring people to their place of work. He name-dropped a B-list British actor and his model girlfriend as we approached the door. 'They're my friends. I brought them here,' he said.

'She's the director at the Club,' he told the doorman.

'Get a haircut,' the doorman replied.

Inside, he secured a table and ordered us a terrifying concoction served in a plastic treasure-chest belching dry ice.

'We'll share it, *Lady and the Tramp*-style,' he said, sticking two straws in.

It was too loud for real conversation. 'How old are you anyway?' he shouted over the pounding RnB.

'I'm thirty.'

'You don't look thirty.'

'People always think they have to make you feel better about your age when you're a girl.'

'I'm twenty, nearly twenty-one.'

'You're a baby.'

'Very patronising, thank you.'

The place began to fill with braying blondes and oily men in jackets worn over black rhinestone T-shirts, who pour into London's centre every night of the week, funnelled through doorways of clubs and bars for a few sticky hours before getting spat back onto the street. I felt a sudden claustrophobic need to get out of the West End.

'Time to go,' I told him, through a daze of alcohol and sugar.

'We should talk soon,' he said, outside the door.

'Sure thing,' I said, spotting my bus rumbling down Piccadilly. 'Thanks for the drink.'

'I'll call ya,' he shouted as I ran across the road.

Kristian was pulling a tray of flapjacks from the oven when I got back to the boat.

'Where have you been?' he asked, dropping the tray onto the stove.

'I got kidnapped by our audition.'

I told him about the dancer waiting for me at the stage door. 'He wants to work at the Club but not as a performer. He'd rather run the show.'

'Sounds like trouble.'

'He will be in five years.'

'Careful.' Kristian sounded unconvinced despite a mouthful of flapjack.

'I'm not going to *do* anything,' I said. 'And don't look at me in that tone of voice.'

'Mmm-hmm.'

'I'm going to have a bath now.'

I sat on the edge of the stained bathtub as it filled. It sat at a wonky angle which I'd never been sure was due to the tide, or if it was sinking into the floor.

In the damp-ravaged mirror I looked critically at my wan face and bruised eyes, under which sleepless nights had smeared permanent charcoal shadows. Turning off the taps, I stepped into the water and lay back with a view of the mouldy ceiling.

My phone announced the arrival of a message, followed by two more in quick succession. I knew before I read them who they'd be from.

Cool to meet you tonight xx

Lets meet soon.

What you doing now?

I thought of Kristian's warning. He was right, of course. Beneath the water, my limbs floated like pale roots.

I'm in the bath :) I messaged back.

A blur of nights and broken mornings. I woke to my alarm, ashes in my mouth and burning in my nose, and hauled myself out of bed. I splashed water on my face and threw on some clothes, downing a pint of water as if I could wash the party out of me.

I left the boat, my new Celine sunglasses shielding me from the harsh sunlight.

From the river, I caught the bus to Victoria Station where I changed onto the Underground, noise battering my senses as the carriage hurtled through sooty tunnels. I put my earphones in then took them out again, music was no help.

At Highbury and Islington, I took an Overground train headed East beyond the borders of Zone 2. Rocked by the train, I closed my eyes and tried to decipher the garbled messages of my heart.

Magda. It felt unreal I'd be seeing her again. She'd been, in many ways, the beginning of everything. Her arm around me that first night in the cloakroom, she told me: '*I want you to be my dancing girl.*' I hadn't known what she meant, but said there was nothing I wanted more. A few weeks later I'd found myself on my way to Glastonbury, with a ticket that said *Performer*, bound for a wild party on the outskirts of the festival run by New Age travellers and squatter punks, where adventurous festival-goers came to gamble in rented tuxedos and gowns. My job was to help in the costume department, and to dance on the stage at night. A week at the festival, awake for days, out of my mind on MDMA and tequila, happier than I'd ever been. Finally, I'd found it. The secret door to the world I'd always known existed, that had nothing to do with anything I'd been taught about the shape a life must take. And every night at midnight, the feeling when I stepped onto stage, of *Her* coming to life. Though she didn't have a name back then. The faces of the grinning audience, carried to the bar on a wave of compliments, showered in fake champagne. The sense of absolute certainty. I didn't take my costume off all the time I was there, sleeping in it, adding another layer of make-up and glitter each day; a grubby, twatted child at a grown-up fancy dress party.

I moved in with Magda after that, into her squat in a former doctor's surgery off the Kingsland Road. Sunken in that way of abandoned buildings, a low, crippled thing surrounded by a shallow moat from the overflow of the blocked drains, at the end of a muddy path bordered by tangles of scrappy undergrowth.

It was not a nice squat. Sad and dirty before it ever became truly sad and dirty, but I chose not to see it. Magda's room the glowing hearth of that run-down place. Wherever she put down, be it festival, truck or ruin, she travelled with a camel train of busted trunks and bulging laundry bags stuffed with fabric. Tattered velvet curtains, a leopard print bedcover, metal candlesticks, costumes and bundles of fake flowers. She'd set to work on a space and despite the interruptions of those who came to call, it would be transformed into a ragtag boudoir where anyone was welcome: the shifty, handsome guys with metal teeth, the shivering junkie needing a warm corner. Spaced-out, teenage ravers seeking entertainment and company. 'My darrrling!' She'd greet them, rolling her Slavic-Rs. 'My *milacik*!' And fold them in her skinny-armed embrace that smelled of perfume, smoke and sweat. She'd sit them on the sofa while she chattered and fetch them a glass or a plate of whatever she had to spare: £4 bottles of red wine, a crumbling spliff, sweet cake from the corner shop. I'd perch wide-eyed, basking in her warmth, though I must have known I did not truly belong in her world. Unlike most people living at the squat, there were other places I could go.

At Hackney Wick, I walked towards London Fields where Magda told me she was living in a hostel. As I approached, it occurred to me that I should have brought her a present.

Walking along the road at the side of the park, I saw a thin figure coming towards me. Her appearance registering in a series of shocks, but the smile was still hers.

We folded each other into a hug. Her arms were fragile, but she smelled the same. I searched her eyes for signs of chemical distortion but saw only a pale, clear blue.

'My babe, it's you,' she said.

The hostel wasn't as bad as I'd feared, a converted Victorian house with a sign in the lobby banning alcohol and drugs from the building, cheap carpet on the stairs. She took me up to her sparsely decorated flat, a leopard-print throw on the sofa, plastic flowers in a vase. An inflatable dingy in the middle of the floor.

'Have you taken the boat out yet?' I said.

'Not yet,' Magda said. 'We'll go next time.'

I hadn't been there long, when her face seemed to crumple, and she ran from the room.

I heard a toilet flush from down the hall and Magda came back, her hands holding her stomach.

'Is it your pain?' I asked. 'Are you seeing a doctor?'

She waved her hand as if batting the words away. 'Fucking useless. They gave me an operation.' She pulled down the front of her trousers to show me the scars on her abdomen, vivid against her milky skin. 'It didn't do nothing.'

'You should go back. Maybe there's something else they can do.'

She didn't reply. Instead, she told me about her boyfriend, who lived at the hostel.

'He's younger than me.' She winked. 'He's beautiful but a very sad boy.'

'Our babies.' She gestured to a small cage on the floor. Inside, squirming in a nest of paper, was a litter of baby mice. 'My boyfriend's crazy about them.'

I looked at the pink and white furry things in the bottom of the cage.

Her face distorted again, and she rushed from the room.

'Ow . . . ow,' I heard from down the hall.

I walked over to the window and looked out at the park.

An ice-cream van was parked next to the gate. The flat was hot and smelled vaguely of sawdust mixed with mouse urine.

'Babe,' I called out. 'Do you want to go to the park? I'll get us an ice cream.'

Outside, the sun was high in the sky. I bought us lollies in the shape of rockets, and we sat together on the grass. She was still beautiful, I saw, her hair no longer skunky, hanging long and limp down her back. Her skin was puffy and slightly translucent, her crooked nose the same. Not yet forty.

I asked her if she'd seen any of the old faces, and she said that she had, but was vague on the details. We'd only been there a few minutes before she doubled over and ran back to use the toilet.

I sat holding her lolly, the coloured syrup dripping on the grass. After twenty minutes, I walked back to the hostel and Magda buzzed me in.

Upstairs, a willowy boy with the face of a saint and scars on his wrists, was sitting on the floor. He said a soft hello and went back to playing with the baby mice. Magda told me she hadn't made it in time and had to squat down in the front garden. She asked if I could go to the shop for her and gave me a short list of things she needed.

I walked down to the corner shop where I put what she'd asked for in the basket: cake, custard, jam. I added basic groceries to the basket, imagining future meals. At the counter, I asked for the tobacco she'd requested and paid on my card.

At the flat, Magda busied herself in the kitchen area, fixing bowls of cake and custard. I put her money back on the table and sat on a chair, watching dust dancing in the sunlight through the window. I searched for something to say, but to make light of her situation seemed cruel. To talk about it even crueller. There was no air in the flat.

Magda handed me a bowl. 'Taste it, it's delicious!'

I looked at it and felt sick, ashamed of my disgust. I lifted the spoon and tasted powdered eggs and sugar.

At the door, I told her I loved her.

'I love you, babe. Come back and see me. Please.'

'I promise,' I said. It was the last time I saw her alive.

Outside, the afternoon sun was low in the sky as I walked to the station in a daze. I tried to think about Magda, but none of the parts seemed to fit. Baby mice. The boat on the floor. What had I expected? Not that, not the end; damage irreversible.

Back when I'd met her, we all did so many drugs I didn't realise the way Magda used them was different. I couldn't remember a time she hadn't talked about her 'pain', gesturing to her abdomen, a stabbing ache. She said it was her womb, her accent blurring the W into a V. It wasn't widely known then that ketamine was addictive, or that it could ravage your kidneys and bladder.

As time went on, being with Magda had taken on the strange aspect of communicating with someone on the other side of the veil, both there but not there, her eyes glazed, nose gritty, her speech and movement out of joint. Sometimes I'd go down to join her in her weird netherworld. 'Hay-low, my beauty,' she'd purr and we'd touch each other's faces, entwined on the floor.

Friends started to distance themselves. I'd left the squat when it got too grim to pretend anymore and found a better place to stay. I still saw Magda but each time things had got worse, her conversation a catalogue of misfortune and, later, horror. 'He raped me, actually,' she told me once, about a man who'd stolen from her. She said it in a matter-of-fact way as I sat on her bed reeling.

The afternoon I finally let go, I'd gone to visit her at her latest temporary home. Not wanting to go inside, I waited on the corner nearby. After half an hour, I called her phone.

'I'm coming, babe,' Magda said. 'I'm on my way.'

More time passed and I called again. 'I'll be there soon, I'm coming.'

For the next two hours I kept calling and Magda kept coming, but she never came.

Loving an addict is to watch someone sinking. You hold out your hands, but they just smile at you. They've already decided.

It wasn't fair. None of it was fair, but fairness has nothing to do with the story you're handed. It has nothing to do with who is weak or strong. It comes to this. For all her light, Magda had little else. When she slipped there was nothing there to catch her.

Chapter 12

Everyone at the Club was fucking. There were people fucking in the toilets, in dark corners and up against the wall on the Beach, and for those seeking privacy there was always the costume department, where you could tangle amongst the rails in the jangle of hangers and the slapping of rubber fetish wear. One night, Russella was coerced into standing guard while a former It girl-turned-call girl serviced a client on the four-poster bed.

I, however, was not fucking anyone. Almost without my realising, the Club had killed my love life stone dead. I rarely ventured out beyond its walls and those revellers who came each night, with their clouded eyes that scanned you like they were measuring something, were not for me. And though I hated to admit it, I was lonely. If the nights were a fever-dream, my days at the Club were curiously stark, coloured by a disquiet that was partly my endless hangover but there were other shadows there too. Half-formed thoughts of my grandmother who called all the time, who I had not been to see. Thoughts of Magda. No time to dwell on any of this, my job a treadmill – the show would not wait – and I found myself craving a warm someone to curl into at the end of a long night. To be held, sometimes, would be enough.

And so, I looked around at what was available, and I liked Enzo's strong arms and the way he made me cocktails. Having made up my mind, it wasn't long before I'd nursed my crush into a full-blown fantasy. The only problem was, Enzo didn't seem to notice the new change of gear.

'What's wrong with him?' I complained to Kristian, as we sat sorting through the boxes in the prop cupboard.

'Maybe he's shy,' Kristian said, wiping down a sticky-looking dildo with antibac.

'He doesn't seem shy.'

Enzo had taken to ambushing me as I walked through the Club after hours, scooping me into a fireman's lift and depositing me back where I started. 'Thank you,' I'd say. 'This is exactly where I wanted to be.'

'He might be worried you'll turn him down.' Kristian put the now-clean dildo into the box labelled 'Sex Toys' and picked up a pair of handcuffs. 'Should I put these in Sex Toys or Weapons?'

'Help me,' I whined.

He sighed. 'You could make the first move.'

'What if he turns me down?'

'Oh, *come on.*'

'Okay, okay,' I said, holding up my hands.

'Ruby?' Calypso, the events manager, stuck her head around the door.

'Everything okay?'

'Delling, we've got a meeting with the vodka people.'

'Did I know about it?' Calypso's turbo-fuelled networking skills didn't always translate to the imparting of certain essential details.

'Come on, they're waiting.'

'I'll come back and help you finish these,' I said to Kristian, who would have them in order and back on their shelves by the time I was released.

*　　*　　*

In the main room, Calypso greeted vodka reps like old friends. I despised these pitch meetings and briefs from corporate clients who didn't know a fire performer from a flower arrangement, their enthusiasm antagonising my hangovers like an over-lit room. To add insult to injury, corporate shows required a 'PG rating' and extra rehearsal time to de-fang and de-claw the numbers, which only added to my resentment.

'Ruby, these guys have come up with an amazing concept for the launch.'

'*So* good,' the fluttering blonde woman was saying to a man in a pinstripe suit. 'It will literally be gold.'

'Triple-distilled through gold pipes,' the vodka man said. 'Our product will be the ultimate in luxury spirits. Our idea is to take the best of your show—'

'Obviously, toned down a little,' said the PR.

'We'll give Rose the night off,' Calypso winked.

'And . . .' The vodka man paused dramatically. 'We do it in gold.'

'You want the costumes to be gold?' I asked.

'Everything,' he said.

'Like the boy in the hoop,' the PR giggled. 'The sexy one.'

She was referring to the Club's recent acquisition of an aerialist moonlighting from Cirque du Soleil.

'You want *him to be* gold?'

'And his hoop,' said the vodka man.

'A gold ring,' sighed the PR.

'We'd have to ask the performers if they're happy to be painted.'

'Yes, well, they're getting paid,' said Calypso who disliked logistics.

'And we can't spray equipment that doesn't belong to us.'

The vodka people looked confused. This wasn't how meetings were supposed to go.

'We can iron out the details later,' said Calypso soothingly.

'When's the event?' I asked.

'The week after next. I told you.'

'We haven't mentioned the private dance,' said the vodka man.

'We're thinking something gold-themed,' said the PR.

'Goldfinger, Golden Eye, golden er . . .' the vodka man riffed, snapping his fingers.

Balls, I thought.

'Eagle,' the vodka man beamed. He turned to me. 'What are your ideas?'

My ideas. A decreasing asset these days, increasingly hard to dredge inspiration from the sludge inside my head. I improvised some nonsense from a ragbag of references, and they proclaimed themselves delighted.

Enzo was behind the bar in the VIP, examining a bottle of the golden vodka.

I pointed at it accusingly. '*That* is about to ruin my life for the next two weeks.'

'You and me both, Madame. I don't get paid extra for corporates.'

I collapsed against the bar.

'You okay?' he said.

My forehead made a sticky sound as it peeled off the counter. 'Remind me why we do this? You speak three languages, what's your excuse?'

'I'm a lazy bastard.' He grinned. 'Want to try some of this fool's gold?'

'That fool's gold costs more than some performers earn in a week.'

'And it will get you drunk.'

'Then yes.'

He poured us each a shot. It tasted a lot like vodka, and we drank some more to make sure.

'I've got an audition now,' I said, slurring only slightly.

'Then god speed you, Madame.'

'Do you want to watch? It's *shibari*. Japanese rope-bondage.'

'An audience at our own private fetish show?'

'Is that a yes?'

There was no sound in the main room but for the breathing of the girl suspended from the central dome. Bound by her partner in an intricate arrangement of knots, her breasts, stomach and thighs bulged sensually around the pressure of the ropes.

'Lower,' the *shibari* master said. When they'd arrived, he'd been softly spoken, almost shy, but now his voice carried a distinct note of command.

I nodded to Enzo, to whom I'd given the task of raising and lowering the winch, pleased to see him out of his comfort zone.

'Down?' he mouthed.

'Slowly,' I mouthed back.

The winch began to descend. When the girl was at waist level, her partner began to rearrange the knots, turning her in the air to change her position. He caressed her gently and she let out a whimper of pleasure.

'Higher,' the *shibari* master said.

The girl ascended once more, and he gave her a gentle spin, her body rotating like a sculpture. In the semi-darkness the room crackled with erotic charge.

I walked over to Enzo and said in a low voice. 'Not bad for a Tuesday afternoon.'

The *shibari* master stowed his equipment away while his partner was getting changed. When she came back down, we discussed the logistics of staging the number on a busy night. It was an odd feeling, making small talk after witnessing such an intimate exchange. We pencilled a date for their debut, and they thanked us politely and left holding hands.

'That's a happy couple,' I said, watching them go.

'I totally agree,' said Enzo.

It was my last audition of the day and we decided to go for dinner. Enzo took me to an exquisite Japanese restaurant off Tottenham Court Road, where we ordered a vast quantity of sashimi, washed down with sake and beer.

'This is on me,' he said, removing a wallet bulging with used notes. 'Tips,' he said, by way of explanation.

After dinner, we moved on to a secret cocktail bar in Chinatown, where he knew all the bartenders by name.

'We're a band of brothers,' he said. 'In service to the morons of the world.'

Kiss me, I thought.

He hadn't recovered his composure since the audition and was babbling a little. *He* is *nervous*, I thought. *Well that's okay*. Emboldened by vodka, I looped my arms around his neck and felt him freeze.

Leaning in to seek his lips, I found them pressed tightly shut. I pulled back. 'No?'

'Madame,' he said. 'It makes perfect sense, I know, but . . .'

I let go of his neck and sat back in my seat.

'Trust me,' he said. 'It would be a disaster. I'm jealous, and you . . .'

'And me what?'

'Maybe it would be amazing. For a month. If we're lucky maybe two. But then you'd hate me and I'd hate you.' He gestured between us. 'This is good, why fuck it up?'

'Not very exciting of you.'

'I'm too cautious, I know.'

We sat in silence, then his face broke into a grin.

'Consider also,' he said. 'Aren't you perhaps a little old for me?'

He walked me to my bus stop, my head swimming with booze and the feeling of a buzz turning sour.

'You're an idiot,' I told him as I boarded the bus, and he blew me a kiss in return.

I climbed to the top deck and sat by myself at the front. I was glad I was drunk. Usually, I loved buses as moving theatres of the day-to-day, but tonight there was only the pale girl looking back at me from the window's dark glass. Even with her face bathed in shadow I could see she looked tired. Older. I'd never thought it would happen. Outside the London night moved by, bright lights and traffic blaring. All the symbols of a city that didn't care either way.

'Number Two's thighs are wobbly,' Sophie whispered in my ear. 'And Number Eight's got struggle-booty.'

The vodka event required a new solo dance, performed in private for anyone willing to spend five hundred pounds on a bottle of the golden vodka. I'd refused Calypso's idea of using one of the dancers, insisting on additional budget to pay someone specifically for the purpose. The last-minute call-out had been surprisingly effective, with two dozen hopefuls showing up at the allotted hour, whom we'd corralled in the VIP. As a peace gesture, I'd asked Lila to assist, but hadn't counted on the rest of the dancers showing up. They'd arranged themselves in a row, X Factor-style on one of the sofas.

'She's hot,' Sophie gestured to a gamine brunette at the end of the line.

'She looks kind of flat-chested?' said Kitty.

'What do you think?' I asked Lila.

'Number Five is a little behind, but she looks great. Seven is amazing but . . .'

'Butter face?' giggled Kitty.

I frowned, but knew she was right. I stood to address the line of waiting girls. 'Three, Five, if you could stay behind, the rest of you are free to go. Thank you, ladies.'

For the final round, Lila taught them a routine from one of the Openers which ended in the usual breast-bearing strip.

Number Three raised a hand. 'I didn't realise we'd be asked to show skin?'

'It was in the call-out,' I said.

'My friend told me about the audition . . .' She looked at me pleadingly.

'Sorry,' I said. 'But it's part of the show.'

Behind me the dancers sniggered.

'Don't do it if you're not comfortable,' I added.

She nodded. 'Well, thanks for seeing me.'

She left the stage, leaving only the brunette who gave us a brilliant smile.

'What's your name?' I said.

'Beatrice.'

'Beatrice, how are you feeling about the routine?'

'I'm down,' she said. 'Let's do it.'

She completed the routine with only a few missteps. She had, the dancers all agreed, a beautiful pair of breasts.

'Congratulations,' I told her. 'Welcome to the Club.'

As everyone was filing out, Enzo appeared in the doorway in his best waistcoat, carrying two ice creams that dripped down his wrists.

'Bye, babe,' Sophie cooed, as the dancers trooped giggling from the room.

Enzo handed me one of the melting cones and we sat down on the stage.

'What's this, an apology?' I said.

'No, it's vanilla.'

'Don't be a dick.'

'Okay. An apology. Why not?'

I looked at him and felt suddenly very weary.

I raised my cone in defeat. 'Why not.'

We touched ice creams and a large blob fell on my shoe.

After a manic fortnight that turned rehearsals into a relay race, the night of the vodka launch arrived. The main room had been brightly lit, making it feel smaller and revealed the shabby state of the decor. A bizarre contraption of gilded pipes like a distillers' laboratory crossed with a plumbing disaster, was mounted on the bar where the bartenders had formed a production line. The guests began to arrive; representatives from the alcohol industry, a smattering of B-list celebs for kudos. I stood on the sidelines watching Calypso flit among the crowd, delighted to see them all. My eyes strayed to the back of the room where Enzo was sliding glasses along the bar like a well-oiled machine.

The PG version of the show limped out and I saw how patchy the gold make-up looked beneath the harsh lights, the costumes hurriedly made. Watching the dancers pull a man onto stage and cover his cheeks with girlish kisses, I wondered what Gabriel Grosse would say. I imagined him storming in, calling everyone 'whores'. Part of me wished he would.

Upstairs in the VIP, Beatrice would be performing her dance of the seven veils. The only thing I'd been able to think of that fitted the 'interactive' brief while avoiding her having to touch anyone. Years before, as a newbie performer, I'd been offered an extra one hundred pounds by a man with three Ferraris in his drive, to perform 'sansculotte'. I'd said no, but I'd considered it. Remembering now, I hoped Beatrice was okay. The evening felt out of joint, or perhaps it was just my mood. The long night stretched ahead of me, and I reached for a drink as a tray swung past.

The launch ended when the doors were opened to the public and the lights dimmed to signal the start of the real party. Some of the drink reps took advantage of finding themselves inside, staying as the room began to fill with a different kind of crowd.

I was propping up the bar with Keen Nasim and a tall man in white robes. Named 'Keen' for his role as the ultimate Club fanboy, he referred to the staff as 'family', lavishing them with dinners and gifts. He introduced his companion as his Guru, a towering Sikh who on closer inspection appeared to be Caucasian and spoke in a Californian drawl. Vodka high, I heard myself agreeing to accompany them to an after-hours members' club off Piccadilly and we took a taxi around the corner.

The club was hidden in a cul-de-sac, bordered by Mayfair establishments with colonial-sounding titles. Keen Nasim pushed me forward as an offering to the icy woman on the door – 'she's the director at the Club' – and we were ushered into the interior, which was moody with dark wood and leather. There was an elegant, compact bar and I went to it directly.

'What can I get you?' the bartender said.

'Is it free?'

'Free with a kiss.' He grinned, and I leant across the bar.

'Why would you do that?' Keen Nasim seemed shocked for a man who spent his nights at the Club.

'For a cocktail,' I said, though this was only partly true.

Behind the bar was a secret room with a hatch through which drinks were served. Much later, I found myself inside with Keen Nasim and the Guru, along with Charlie and Lila who'd arrived with Beatrice in tow. We were crowded around a table, chaotic with glasses and the paraphernalia of a night that should have ended hours before.

'I'd like to get to know you,' Charlie was saying, presumably for Lila's benefit.

'Why?' I asked, but he couldn't say.

On my other side, the Guru was explaining the theory of the universe in terms of sacred geometry and sketching a picture on a napkin. 'In the beginning, there was only the awareness of awareness, and the awareness was male,' he said. 'Then one day he created a female being inside himself, so that he could know himself. This is mirrored in relationships when the woman becomes the mirror of the man's subconscious.'

144

I was tuning him out, observing Beatrice in deep conversation with Lila. I recognised her dazzled expression. She belonged to the Club now.

The Guru had moved on to the nature of the soul. 'It's kind of like a doughnut pulling itself through its own hole. Except the hole is a lot smaller than that, so really, it's shaped more like an apple. Or a pomegranate. And of course, there are aspects to it that are more like a fig, but that's another thing entirely.'

God I was bored. But the effort it would take to extricate myself and make my escape was beyond me. I did another line in the hope it might spur me into action.

Later, after the Guru had confided he knew the secret of the full-body orgasm, I found myself sitting next to Lila. 'I really missed you,' she was saying, her eyes wet with emotion.

You little psycho, I thought.

I took her hand. 'I missed you too.'

We stayed until the cleaners arrived. When, finally, we left the secret room, we found the bar empty and the club closed for the night. Stepping into the day, the sunlight burned like pale fire.

Greeting the morning after an all-nighter can feel like a triumph, and sometimes a catastrophe. Veering between the two, I wobbled in the direction of my bus stop. Piccadilly was already bustling with morning traffic and caffeinated people walking fast.

'Ruby,' a voice called out behind me.

Charlie was standing next to a taxi, Lila and Beatrice already inside. 'Can we drop you somewhere?' In the bright light of morning, he looked close to death.

'I'm taking the bus.'

'Really?' He sounded amazed.

I gave what I hoped was a debonair shrug and waved as they drove away. As the taxi receded, Lila turned to look at me through the rear-view window and for a moment I saw myself through her eyes, alone and wasted in the street.

Chapter 13

October's end was fast approaching, the Club gearing itself towards the annual Halloween ball. I'd gone all-out, hiring a string quartet for the VIP and creating several new numbers, my love for the spooky season having no bounds. A job lot of pumpkins had arrived, turning the main room into a sea of orange, which Kristian and Archie spent hours carving into elaborate designs no one would ever see.

On stage, a boy was assembling a steel Cyr Wheel, a visually stunning piece of kit roughly two metres in diameter that turns its rider into Leonardo's *Vitruvian Man*, made flesh. Our last audition of the day. He'd come prepared, in ghoulish clown make-up, shorts and braces like a deranged schoolboy. I cocked an eye at the stage's low concrete ceiling when he expressed his intention to fire-breathe inside the wheel.

'I assume you're insured?'

'Of course.' He smiled, showing blacked-out teeth.

Archie finished assisting with the set-up and joined me on the sofa to watch.

'What's he doing?' he said, when the boy hoisted himself into the lighting rig.

I said nothing as the lights dimmed, eerie music drifting over the speakers.

My phone vibrated in my hand, and I glanced down and felt my stomach flip when I saw the name on the screen: *Trouble*.

The Dancer's messages had increased in frequency over the previous weeks, little flutters along the lines of: *What you up to?* A mixture of flattery and teasing. I'd kept my replies brief, busy being important but with a spark of something else. Waiting.

Auditions, I messaged back, and caught Archie glance over in irritation.

There was a thud as the boy came tumbling onto stage, landing flat on his face in a perfect pratfall. I caught my breath. Auditions could be anything from the curious to the cringe-worthy, but occasionally they were thrilling.

He peeled himself off the floor and began to caper, his drooling leer obscuring his wholesome good looks. He lifted the vast wheel with both hands and gave it a firm push, sending it spinning, light glinting from the polished steel.

Catching it with both hands, he spun it again and hopped inside, bracing against the hand and footholds on the inner edge. Using his core, he manipulated the wheel at the centre of the stage, occasionally lifting his lower body outside, following the trajectory of the turn.

'We'll have to make room in the Halloween show,' I said. 'He's amazing.'

On stage, the boy was gathering momentum, his body and the hoop a silver blur, and for a moment I was there with him, suspended in the eye of the storm.

Slowing down, he leaped from the wheel leaving it turning, to swig from a bottle of Jack Daniel's containing his fuel. Lighting a small, wick-ended torch, he jumped back inside and, when he'd got it on an even keel, readied himself and released a spray of fuel into the torch's flame.

A ball of fire like a mushroom cloud billowed towards us. It rolled across the stage's ceiling, tongues of flame licking the velvet curtains, and my face was blasted with heat as the boy staggered backwards from the wheel.

I stood up when his hands flew to his face as the wheel fell to the stage with a metallic clang. The smell of burning hair stung the air.

'Shit,' I said. 'Are you okay?'

He lowered his hands. 'I'm okay.'

He was smacking his lips, thoughtfully. Stepping closer, I could see they were blistered, a fine coating of black soot around his mouth.

'Was that normal?'

'No,' he shook his head. 'That wasn't the right fuel.'

The information registered in a series of shocks. I turned to Archie, who looked pale.

'I changed it.' His voice was strangled.

'You did what?'

'I thought the other stuff would be too smoky.'

'You changed the fuel without telling him?' I stared at him.

'I'm sorry.'

'It's cool,' the boy called from the stage. 'No harm done.'

'It is not fucking cool,' I hissed at Archie.

'I'm sorry,' he said again. He looked suddenly very young.

'Go and get some ice,' I said. 'You could have killed him.'

I turned to the boy. 'I can't apologise enough.'

'Did you want me to do it again?'

'Absolutely not.'

'Have I got the job then?'

I offered the boy a fortnight's contract at a higher rate of pay. I figured he'd more than earned it. He bid me good-bye with apparently no hard feelings, and I went to find Kristian.

149

'So, we nearly killed our audition,' I said walking into the prop cupboard.

'I just saw Archie,' Kristian said. 'He's pretty shaken.'

'He should be.' I sat down on a chair and rubbed my eyes. 'Amazingly, the boy still wants to work here.'

'What would've happened if he'd been hurt?'

I thought of the sleazy inspector from the local fire brigade whose visits included a seat at one of the VIP tables, complimentary champagne, and a clutch of hostesses for company. 'I imagine management has its own way of dealing with things.'

It rained all week, and it was still raining on the morning of the Halloween ball. I sulked around the boat, stepping over the saucepans on the kitchen floor, put there to catch the leaks that sprung as fast as Kristian could patch them. I'd always known Halloween as a two-week bonanza of gigs and parties, catching up with friends in dressing rooms across the city. So much better than Christmas. But this year I found I could not locate my seasonal cheer.

I rifled through my wardrobe searching for inspiration for the ball, stopping when I came to a white catsuit inherited from a music video shoot. It had sheer panels and frills, with kinky detailing in the form of an industrial metal zipper on the crotch, which ran from front to back. I removed it from the hanger and felt a little better.

That evening, avoiding Archie, I got ready in the performers' dressing room. Channelling *A Clockwork Orange*, I'd completed the look with platform boots, a bowler hat and cane. Applying a single spidery eyelash, I stepped back to admire the result. In the mirror, a former version of myself looked back at me. I was pleased to see her. That girl had known how to have fun.

The Cyr Wheel boy was getting ready nearby. He smiled at me from behind his clown make-up. 'I wouldn't have recognised you.'

'This is the real me,' I told him.

'It's really cool.'

'Your make-up's neater tonight.'

'Do you want me to change it?'

I grinned in response, reached out and smeared both hands down his face. 'Much better,' I said.

Then twirling my cane, I tipped my hat and went down to watch the show.

White light strobed from inside the television set, thick smoke billowing across the stage. It crept over the edge, smothering the Club in its sickly, chemical smell.

From inside the television a twisted figure appeared, bent backwards Exorcist-style. Pushing through a slit in the black cloth of the screen, the contortionist in the dirty white nightie crawled from the television, her head peering at a horrible angle between her legs. Unravelling her body inch by inch until she was standing upright, she glared one-eyed at the audience through the black hair that fell across her face.

Another body appeared – Fancy, in an identical costume – followed by another and another, until five little girls in stained white nighties and black wigs swayed, backlit and wreathed in smoke at the edge of the stage. They moved through the crowd like sleepwalkers, headed for the central podium.

Pushing my way forward, I looked up at the dome expecting to see the winch lowering to meet them.

Come on, Archie.

On the central podium, the girls formed a circle around Fancy as the audience gathered round. The winch hadn't moved.

Come on.

Finally, it began to descend as the music reached its thundering conclusion – and ended.

Silence like a vacuum in the absence of applause filled the room. It was only a few moments but they felt like minutes.

'That was *The Ring*! Happy Halloween, my babies!' Athena rallied the crowd's attention back to the party as the lights switched into party mode.

I caught Fancy's baleful expression as the girls hurried from the podium. 'Fuck,' I swore under my breath. 'Fuckfuckfuckfuckfuck.'

I stormed backstage and found Archie in the prop cupboard.

'Are you going to mention completely fucking the finale in your show report?' I demanded.

'I couldn't see them,' he said. 'There was too much smoke.'

'There was an audio cue, don't you listen in rehearsals?' I had my hands on my hips.

'I couldn't start the winch until it was safe,' he said coldly. 'The audience don't care. They won't even remember tomorrow.'

'It doesn't mean we do a shit job,' I said, furious with myself as much as him.

I went to the bar, where Enzo whistled at my catsuit then lined up tequila shots in commiseration. Around me, the audience staggered and swayed, the show already forgotten.

Archie was right, they didn't care. But I was bereft, robbed of the high I'd been counting on to carry me through the night. I'd knocked back my second shot when I felt my phone vibrate.

Where you?

A smile crept over my lips. *Just finished the show*, I messaged back.

Come to a party.

When?

Pick you up in 20.

'Gotta go,' I told Enzo, taking one more shot for the road.

His face darkened. 'Enjoy, Madame,' he said. 'Happy Halloween.'

I waited by the statue of Eros on the corner of Piccadilly, with a head full of tequila. All around me bloodied ghosts and ghouls were howling their way to parties all over town, my own spirits riding high on a wave of liquor. I was free, if only for the night, to get lost in a story of my own.

A taxi pulled up at the lights. 'Is that you?' said a voice from the open window.

Twirling my cane, I opened the door and swung myself into the cab.

'Trouble,' I said, doffing my hat.

The Dancer looked nervously at my costume.

'I'm a Droog,' I explained.

'You look very nice,' he said, sounding almost prim.

'Where's your costume?' He was wearing jeans with grubby Converse All Stars.

He pulled a gas mask from his pocket and held it to his face. 'Scary enough for ya?'

'Yes, actually,' I said. 'So, where are we going?'

The taxi took us to Knightsbridge, dropping us off outside a set of imposing metal gates. Beyond them, the darkness of Hyde Park. I'd heard rumours of the secret party that happened somewhere inside when the West End clubs had closed for the night.

The Dancer made a phone call, dancing impatiently on the spot. 'He's not picking up,' he said, walking over to the gates with their crown of evil-looking spikes. Bracing a rubber sole against the bars, he began to push himself up.

'What are you doing?' A man was walking towards us on the other side.

'All right, mate, I tried to call ya.'

The man unlocked the gate. 'Not very fucking discreet.'

The Dancer grinned, pulling him into a reluctant bro-hug as he hurried us towards the small cottage at the edge of the park.

Inside, a handful people were dancing to House music in the pink glow of a neon strip light in what had once been the living room. Other than the DJ decks and sound system and a makeshift bar, the room was empty of furniture. We procured some drinks – warm rum and ginger in plastic party cups – and stood by the wall, not yet comfortable enough to dance with each other. It was early still, the party not yet started, the atmosphere both illicit and awkward.

'Wait here,' he said and disappeared down a corridor.

I sipped my drink, trying to make sense of the location. How had they got the keys? And how were they getting away with it?

'Come on.' The Dancer had reappeared at my elbow. I followed him to a small room where a group were hunkered over a glass table. The atmosphere in the room was one I associated with the West End crowd – cocaine, sex, with a dash of swingers' party. They eyed us with interest as we sat down.

'Hello, sexy people,' a lady in a leopard-print cat costume said.

'Hello, yourself,' said the Dancer, bending over the table and passing me the note.

'Who are you two, then?' said a man in a black fedora.

'Ruby,' I said, rubbing the sting from my nose.

'She's director at the Club,' said the Dancer.

'Oh yeah?' said the man, as if our story made more sense.

I could feel the desires of the others crowding in around the table – his beauty and me, a possible 'in'. I'll go home, I decided. One more drink then leave.

'I need some air,' I told the Dancer.

'I'll come with.'

Outside in the garden, we found a swing beneath an arbour decorated with fairy lights. We sat down, and I watched him struggle to skin up a joint.

'You do it,' he said, thrusting it towards me.

I finished rolling while he fidgeted and hummed to music that wasn't there.

'Do you like the party then?' he demanded as I passed it back.

'It's okay. The people are a bit creepy.'

'Yeah.' He exhaled a plume of smoke into the night. Then he pulled me to my feet. 'Come on, let's go.'

A teenage thrill shot through my body as we ran from the party across a wide lawn and into the darkness of the trees beyond.

Down broad pathways bathed in shadow, he let go of my hand to put on his gas mask, dancing in front of me, his limbs jerking in disjointed, spidery moves. He had an unsettling energy and I had a shiver of adrenalin at a sudden vision of myself strangled in the rose bushes.

Then we were running again, deeper into the park until we came to a shining, wide-open space where the moon had burnished the grass in silver.

He caught my hands and began to spin me until I screamed like a schoolgirl, and we began to fight, trying to throw each other to the ground. He twisted my arms as I kicked his legs from under him, and we collapsed on the damp grass. I landed on top of him, our faces close together.

And then, because I'd seen the film a thousand times before, I leant down and kissed him.

My head was swimming with a sense of déjà vu as I led him down the pontoons towards the boat.

Forgoing the front door, I let myself in through the hatch into the kitchen. Lowering myself down first, I watched his dirty baseball boots, long legs, and finally the rest of him materialise in front of me.

He looked around at the unfamiliar surroundings. 'Here?' he said, gesturing at the sofa.

I shook my head. 'My cabin's at the end.'

'Do you want me to carry you?'

'Sure?'

Upside-down in a fireman's lift, I heard Felicity let out a squeal of anger as my boots hit her wall. I'd be in the doghouse tomorrow but was enjoying myself too much to care.

He dropped me on the bed, his eyes roaming my cabin, the rusted portholes and glowing lamps, the curios on the dusty shelves. Tomorrow, I'd show him the bullet holes in my bedroom walls.

He looked at me, his face unreadable. Then pulled his shirt over his head, and I had the same punched-in-the-face feeling I'd had when I first met him, with the fleeting thought I'd never sleep with anyone this beautiful again.

Not long after, battling on the springs of my broken bed, there was the sound of an industrial zipper being pulled, and his mocking voice crowing out in the dark.

'Ay, girl, look what I found!'

Chapter 14

Narcissister was upside-down on stage, balancing on her hands to reveal the head that was growing between her legs. Only you could barely see.

'Reg, it's too dark,' I said into the mic.

There'd been another lock-in the night before and the young lighting designer was seriously off his game.

'Sorry, can we go from the top?'

Narcissister came down from her handstand, her peasant skirt falling around her ankles. 'Is there a problem?'

'We just need to get it right.' I tried to keep the cringe out of my voice. Narcissister was a big headliner from New York, and I hated us to appear sloppy. Recently, Reg's work had been getting increasingly more chaotic; afternoons he'd show up sweating, over an hour late, full of apologies. The lifestyle was starting to get to him, but I had a soft spot for the sweet-natured kid, so was persevering with a mix of older-sister sternness, patience and gritted teeth.

My phone buzzed in my back pocket as I cued the music again, my stomach lurching as I read the message: *Me. The Club. Crazy?*

'How's that, Ruby?' Reg called from the lighting desk.

'Uh,' I blinked, attempting to locate myself back in the room. 'Better. Yes.'

*   *   *

After the tech, I went to the toilets and read the message again. *Me. The Club. Crazy?* In the weeks since Halloween, I'd almost managed to forget this uncomfortable detail of the Dancer's interest in me. The forgetting had been easy, and for a while I believe he had too, in the excitement that followed at a daze of parties across the city. Aiming to impress, I'd taken him to shebeens in Dalston where drag queens worked behind the bar, a hidden members' club behind the door of a derelict pub that was decorated with exotic taxidermy animals, warehouse parties in Clapton and Limehouse, and once, a rave on a squatted ship in Docklands; offering him everything I knew about the city. He was greedy for it all, his excitement irresistible; enchanting the strangers we met, his sticky fingers collecting souvenirs along the way: a candlestick, champagne glass, a sword. I was proud showing him off, this dazzling, dancing thing, while uncertain of myself in his reflected light, unsure if it was flattering or tragic in nature. These nights ended with expensive rides on my Addison Lee account, back to the boat where in the twilight of my cabin we had the kind of sex that occurs between those unsure whether the other is friend or foe.

I deleted the message and leant over the sink to study my face in the mirror, my dilated pupils showed black, liquid pools. The signs, I knew, were bad.

Felicity was waiting for me in the VIP. To make things up to her, I'd finally brought her in for a workshop. True to form, she'd gone the extra mile, bringing with her two bulging laundry bags of props.

'Hello, sweet.' I gave her a long hug. 'You came prepared.'

'I've been shopping for my tail.'

'Your tail?'

'*Little Mermaid* fishy-realness.'

'Gabriel Grosse has a thing for Disney.'

'I bought a bubble machine and a treasure chest,' she said, rummaging in one of the bags.

'Gadgets and gizmos aplenty?'

'Uh-huh.' She pulled out a plastic lobster. 'Here's my gadget.' She located an oversized dildo. 'And here's my gizmo, but I can't use it because of my tail, see?'

'I see.'

'So, I take these.' She held up a large pair of scissors. 'And cut it in half.'

'You're not using the dildo, are you?'

'No, darling.' She smiled even wider. 'I'm going to pull a string of pearls out of my va-jay-jay.'

'You haven't done a penetration stunt before . . .' I wracked my brain for alternative endings but found only troubling thoughts of the Dancer.

Felicity smiled wryly. 'Darling, you don't need to spell it out. If the rich and revolting need a new grotesque to ogle, I don't give a flying fuck. Fat is funny, right?'

I gaped at her.

'I know, I know, I'm just so terribly *brave*.'

I laughed, partly from relief. 'We've already got a number with a pearl reveal, how about sushi instead?'

That afternoon, Kristian procured a box of plastic nigiri from a shop in Chinatown which we strung on a length of fishing wire. With enough lube Felicity managed to fit the entire set inside her. The number was christened Sushi Pussy and would make its debut the following week.

Where u?

I'd been drifting off when the message arrived. The screen on my phone said 3 a.m. Groaning, I smashed my face into the pillow, rolled over and watched my fingers message him back.

Boat.

There was a beat, before a warning appeared: *Im coming for u*

A pulse of erotic dread passed through my body ending all possibility of sleep. Feeling I'd made a terrible mistake, I flung my legs out of bed.

The boat was rocking, and I kept one hand on the wall as I made my way to the bathroom. I ran cold water into the sink and splashed my face and neck, then set about applying invisible make-up to make me look alive. Letting my T-shirt and knickers drop to the floor, I stuck my leg up on the side of the bath, borrowing one of the boys' razors, and proceeded to shave everything. Then I brushed my teeth.

After I'd finished, I put on a pair of lace-trimmed shorts and went back to bed. I checked the time on my phone: 3.35 a.m.

An hour passed as I lay awake, waiting. Finally, I heard his footsteps reverberating the length of the boat, the dull thud as his feet hit the kitchen floor.

'Hello,' I said, as he came ducking through the low doorway of my cabin.

'I fell asleep on the bus.' His tone was accusatory. 'I had to get a taxi.'

'Oh.'

'I'm making a brew.'

He stomped back down the corridor towards the kitchen. Much like me, he punctuated life's triumphs and challenges by putting the kettle on. I flopped against my pillow and closed my eyes.

He reappeared a few minutes later with a mug of tea. Ignoring me, he set it down, stripped to his boxers and climbed into bed, hunching over with his back to me.

My temper was rising when his hand grasped my thigh and in one lightning-fast move, flipped me onto my front.

'Do you want me to fuck you?' he said, his weight on my back.

'Yes,' I answered truthfully.

There was a yanking of clothes and a constricted tangle of limbs, and I gripped the mattress with the shock of connection.

'Slow down,' I whispered before he rolled off me, gasping.

I turned around and stared at him. 'Are you kidding me?'

His eyes were closed, a smug smile on his face.

'Next time you wake me up to fuck me for three minutes, stay home and have a wank.'

He looked injured. 'It wasn't three minutes. More like four.'

I let out a sound like a scream and threw a pillow at him, wishing it were something heavier.

Balanced at the edge of the mattress where he sprawled in an arrogant starfish, I lay awake until first light. I wanted him to wake up and fuck me again. I wanted him gone, to never have met him. And though he'd never made me come, my body still flooded with a chemical high at the memory of my hands on the ceiling, legs wrapped around his waist, when the reflection of us in the mirror had taken my breath away. It had looked like the best sex of my life.

Outside the boat, the city would be waking, people on their way to work, by car, bus, on foot. Coffee in takeaway cups, breakfast on the fly. How many others were out there lying sleepless next to another, desperate to make them stay? It was the loss of my power in the situation that shocked me the most. Was it that he was *so* very beautiful, or being surrounded by so much beauty at the Club, where the qualities I'd taken for granted as fascinating – which included the fact of the boat and my crazy friends – got somehow lost in the mix? His wanting gave me back to myself but left me in anguish. Like all drugs, he was both cause and cure.

He woke bursting with rude health, proclaiming hunger. Ashamed and besotted, I dragged myself to the kitchen where I slammed a frying pan on the stove and watched him devour egg after egg. After he'd decimated the contents of the fridge, we climbed onto the roof to sit in the afternoon sun.

'Wanna play a game?' he said.

'No.'

'Come on.' He took my hands and pulled me to my feet. 'You lean back,' he said. 'And I lean back.'

Below us the brown river water churned between the boat's hull and its neighbour. He gripped my hands. We leaned back.

'You've got to trust me,' he said, when I lost my nerve for the second time.

'But I don't.' I sat back down.

'Aw, don't say that Rub-io.'

I lay back and closed my eyes. Sometimes it was easier not to look at him. I felt him run a hand down my calf and pick up one of my feet. The rest of my body disappeared as he began to massage it with firm and practised fingers.

'You trying to get on my good side?'

'It's working,' he laughed.

I opened my eyes a crack. Behind him the sun gave his outline a golden glow, his face intent on what he was doing. Something glinted in his ear, and I recognised a diamanté earring in the shape of a spider that I'd left on a shelf in my cabin and felt pleased he'd stolen a piece of me to wear.

He saw me watching him and his expression became wicked again. 'Wanna go to bed?' he said. 'I'll tuck you in.'

I was early for the company rehearsal so sat on the stage to wait, scrolling through old messages from the Dancer, gleaning new meanings in his digital scattershot, which seemed to follow the zigzagging train of his thoughts. My relationship to my phone had changed since I met him. Before it was a means of communication, a sometimes-toy, now a device for both self-torture and self-soothing. I took a pouting selfie and uploaded it to Instagram, hoping that he'd see. Hashtag: *#work*

The dancers arrived in a gaggle of childlike voices and cheap fashionable clothes; the ink barely dry on their most recent tattoos. New lovers every other week, who came and went unmourned, their lives marred only by the tiny dramas that blew through like squalls; something to pass the time. Less than ten years between us but they made me feel like an elder, embarrassed by my current predicament. What had happened to me?

All through the day and into the night, my phone didn't leave my hand, watching him appear online then disappear again. *Last seen 11.24 p.m.* Who was he talking to? Was he punishing me? *Last seen 1.37 a.m.* Or – the worst thought of all – growing tired of me? In the corridors, on the dance floor and at the bar: drunk and horny people reeling each other in to music that ached and moaned. It was the Club's other currency, half its appeal in the promise of the night's end; the kind of love that leaves stained sheets, sadness and a junk food craving for more.

Maciek was awake when I got home that night, sitting on the living-room floor, deep in his laptop, where he could often be found between the hours of midnight and 6 a.m.

'Maciek, I'm *sad*,' I said, sitting down beside him.

'Mmm,' he said, gazing into his screen.

'Everything hurts,' I said. 'My chest, my stomach . . .'

'You sound Emo.'

'I *am* Emo.'

'It's pretty to be sad.'

'But am I still pretty?' I said before I could help myself.

His eyes slid towards me. '*Gurl*. Just find someone else.'

'You're a Triffid,' I said. 'It's different for you.'

There was a blooping sound, announcing a Skype call.

'It's China,' he said apologetically.

'Tell them I said hi.'

I went back to bed and stalked the Dancer until dawn.

4.35 a.m.

5.15 a.m.

Last seen.

It was a wretched week. In workshops I made desultory numbers, which in some way reflected my state of mind: motifs of sex and violence, lovers tearing each other apart. One afternoon, my grandmother called while I was choreographing an aerial tribute to my own humiliation. 'I'll call you back, GJ,' I told her, watching in dismay as for the next hour my phone continued to flash her name on the screen, sick with guilt that I hadn't seen her.

Then one evening, Maciek knocked on my cabin door with a gift of two VIP wristbands to a secret show the following night, at the shiny white club beneath the Westway. America's newest alt-RnB star, in town for his UK debut.

'Bring someone deserving,' he said wryly.

When he'd gone, I immediately messaged the Dancer and was delighted when he called me back. 'Are you for real?'

'Do you want to come?'

'Ohmygod *yes!*'

I heard him crowing to a friend in the background and I was his sexy older lover again, with keys to the city and more. I told myself it was a peace-offering, a way of assuaging my guilt for refusing him the Club. But really, I just wanted to see him.

We met at the station around the corner from the venue. I'd spent time on my make-up and wore a halter-neck dress that plunged. He turned up high, wearing a shell-suit jacket that might have been manufactured the same year he was born.

The queue stretched around the block. We walked to the front, our wristbands flashing, past hungry eyes that asked: *Take me* and *Why them?* Inside, we joined the crowd of beautiful faces, self-conscious representatives from the intersecting galaxies of fashion, music and clubland, some of them internet famous in a way I was already too old to understand. We hustled our way to the front across the slippery white floor, where once I'd danced for canapés and brown envelopes of cash.

The RnB star took to the stage with a group of session musicians. He seemed surprised to find himself in front of a live audience. His disaffected falsetto reverberated off the walls of the high-ceilinged room, the cool kids nodding their heads and taking pictures with their phones. The Dancer's eyes didn't leave his screen as he filmed every number.

'Why don't you just watch it?' I said, but he ignored me.

After the show, he announced he wanted to go backstage.

'No way,' I said.

'Come on, bet you can talk your way in.'

'What for?'

'For a photo.'

'*No.*'

He looked at me, a malevolent gleam in his eye. 'Why not? You could fuck him.'

I stared at him.

'Go on,' he said. 'Take all of him.'

'Why would you say that to me?'

He shrugged and pouted, unspoken accusations lashing the space between us.

He grinned. 'Maybe we could share you.' He reached out his hand but before I could think, I'd shoved him as hard as I could.

Walking alone up the Portobello Road, foolish in my dress, hot tears blurring my vision, I vowed never to see him again.

He messaged just as I arrived back at the boat. *Thanks for tonight, Rubio x*

My heart's pathetic leap at the sight of the single black X made me wild with fury, then want to cry. Already, I could feel myself adjusting my refusal for something softer.

Was he truly so bad, my lovely tormentor? I'm certain he wasn't. But the power you give another is only as powerful as our notion of how they see us, which really is how we wish to see ourselves. And the power I gave him was mighty because of the girl he, for a brief time, had brought back to life. For he reminded me of myself at twenty, with hunger enough to devour two cities.

I was in the VIP, which had been lit an aquatic blue and green. In the middle of the stage was a large, glittering clamshell. A kiddies' paddling pool with a ten-minute makeover. Over the childlike scene, Felicity's bubble machine spewed pretty rainbow suds.

Felicity emerged from the shell to the sound of crashing waves, a sequin starfish covering each nipple, lip-synching into a dildo. I watched, pride overcoming any lingering concern as she wooed the audience into the palm of her hand, her wide-eyed mermaid turning lascivious with a flick of her tongue, before the curtains swished shut once more, catching briefly on the paddling pool shell.

'Well done, sweets,' I said, handing her a robe backstage as she dropped the plastic sushi into a child's toy bucket.

'I think I used too much lube tonight,' Felicity said. 'They almost popped out early.'

'Lovely.'

She put on the robe, and I walked her down to the dressing room where she removed the starfishes and poured her milky breasts into a gorgeous transparent bra.

'I would like to drink champagne and meet some perverts,' she said.

'And you shall. Come on, Narcissister is about to start.'

We went downstairs to the main room and found our way to the front of the stage, the curtains opening on Narcissister, her face concealed by a mask of feminine humanoid features, a headscarf tied beneath her chin. In her arms she carried a large wicker basket.

She moved in a kind of dance to jaunty Eastern European folk music, reflected in her costume of embroidered apron over large swinging skirts. Suddenly she was interrupted by an electronic distortion, an almost scream, that was accompanied by the sound of a ringing telephone.

Narcissister froze, her head cocked at an angle. Slowly she placed the basket down and began to rummage inside, pulling out an old-fashioned telephone receiver attached to a curling wire. As she held the phone to her ear, Nina Simone's mournful voice came over the speakers like a spell, and my breath caught in my throat.

Love me, love me, say you do.
Let me fly away with you.

Letting the phone slip from her fingers, Narcissister reached beneath her chin to untie the headscarf, removing it along with the mask, to reveal a white headwrap and second mask worn beneath the first; this one with dark brown skin. Falling to her knees she began slowly to polish the basket and then the floor, the headscarf now a rag, her character now the unsettling and familiar figure of a work-worn 'Mammy'.

For my love is like the wind,
And wild is the wind.

I felt wetness on my cheeks as Nina Simone continued to sing, her crying voice reaching like fingers into parts of me that had no words of their own.

From inside the basket, the phone rang again.

Narcissister answered and the music changed, shocking me from my place in the marine darkness.

I wiped the tears from my face as on stage Narcissister unwound the headwrap to free the Afro hidden underneath, now a proud Soul Sista. Woman after woman she became, each one a fragment of her own lineage, the sound of the phone pulling her through space and time until she stood, naked and liberated, as she answered the final call, reaching between her legs to remove the cell phone concealed inside her.

'I'll be back,' I murmured to Felicity.

I was still thinking about love as I pushed my way along the corridor, and another Nina Simone song I used to sing that was a declaration of freedom, of feeling good. But where had that story ended? Here, which was nowhere. A hall of mirrors in the heart of darkness. Bottom of the rabbit hole.

Looming faces, the music and voices too loud, as I made for the Beach, my sanctuary among the rooftops. When I got there, Lila and Beatrice were perched on a wall, smoking in the shadows.

'Whatcha doing?' said Lila when she saw me.

It was too late to go back. 'Just taking a break,' I said and went to sit on the adjacent wall.

Lifting myself up, I remembered my present company and lowered my legs to the floor.

Twin red cherries crackled in the silence before Lila said, 'I met a dancer who knows you,' and the blood curdled in my veins.

She described their meeting at the party in Hyde Park, her words drowned out by a rushing in my head. 'He wants to work with me,' she added.

'Why not?' I said. 'He's good.' Somehow keeping my voice steady, thankful she couldn't see my face in the dark.

I stayed on the wall after they'd gone, waiting for my adrenalin to stop surging, running through each terrible scenario of the Dancer at the Club. It would take less than one rehearsal for Lila to understand everything.

I'd lose him.

I'd never had him.

I knew what I had to do. I would do it calmly and with the minimum of fuss. The only thing now to save from the fire, was to never let him know that I cared.

Chapter 15

'What does it taste like?' the boy asked his friend.

The friend, who was Irish, chewed thoughtfully on the gum I'd pushed into his mouth after removing it from my own.

'It tastes of Ruby,' the Irish boy said.

The VIP was very loud and very boring. Riding a restless mood, I'd met the boys at the bar. 'We're models,' they informed me, full of the uneasy swagger of the young.

'Model-influencer-actor-DJ,' I murmured.

'Huh?'

Reg the lighting tech came sidling over. 'Coming to Hyde Park?' He eyed my new friends cautiously.

'Let's do it.'

'You're leaving?' said the Irish boy.

'I'll give you the address.'

Outside, Reg and I hurried through the rain into a waiting taxi, London a blur of lights as we drove through the city.

My partying had accelerated in the weeks since I'd last seen the Dancer. Sadder than I liked to admit, I'd been cruising the arteries of late-night London, populated by those who have no interest in greeting the day from the safety of a warm bed, my phone pinging until dawn with the hails of others scattered across the city, unwilling for the party to end.

Every so often a text would arrive from an unknown number, the message always the same: *I'm worried about you.*

Don't be, I'd reply.

At the cottage in the park, I immediately lost Reg in the crowd. I wandered the corridors peering around doors, startling those inside who froze in vignettes of contemporary vice.

I ran into some party friends and snorted something from a vial. 'It's not coke, by the way,' they told me after.

'It doesn't matter,' I said.

I floated back to the pink-lit dance floor. Where was Reg? I closed my eyes and began to dance. It felt good just to move, not to think. When I opened them, a man in a V-neck vest, gold tooth flashing, was moving towards me. The drug was hitting my system now, the room around me starting to wobble.

Ah ketamine, my final thought before I tumbled.

Time slows.

The music expands, unfolding like origami

it has surfaces, colour, geometric possibilities,
you reach out to touch, but it changes once more,

crystallises, shatters and

alone in a blue-black space,
suddenly, you understand everything

the building blocks of the universe laid out like Lego
you laugh for not seeing all along,
and it's a laugh of delight because this drug exists to
    show us the way
and all you have to do is rave, is rave, is rave

Wait.
Is that right?

You lose the thread but there's another shining up
    ahead,
it blasts you with white light containing code

you are a brain in a jar,

awareness itself

amoeba

Unsure of where you fit into all of this, you drift on,
there's so much to learn, to remember

A field of purple tulips comes into focus below, petals
    breathing
you hover as they open and close
they're calling you to make love

it is the erotic moment of your life

Somewhere in the distance, you can hear Olivia
    Newton John
singing *let's get physical, physical*

All the answers are here, between the lines

you float towards them and beyond.

The man was too close now, hands on my hips. I stepped
away from him and as I did my dress, fastened at the front
by a dozen tiny buttons, came apart.

'No,' I tried to say, my voice in slow motion.

The gold tooth was receding. Vaguely, I understood I'd been picked up and carried from the dance floor.

'I'm gonna kill him. D'you want me to kill him?' Reg was saying as he set me back on my feet.

'Not his fault. Buttons, see?' I managed, fumbling with my dress, and he gave me the look I usually gave him when he was behaving like a hot mess.

'Don't,' I shook my head. 'Buttons.'

A wave of nausea came over me. I raised a finger and ran for the door.

Vomiting in the flowerbed outside, I tasted booze and spearmint chewing gum. My mouth filled with saliva as the drug's trace repeated and I retched again, a seemingly endless stream of watery bile splattering the geraniums.

The world still spinning, I sat on the wet grass and rested my head on my knees.

Not your finest hour.

Oh, leave me alone.

It was getting light when I stumbled from the cottage, a low mist creeping across the park. There was only so long you could chase a good time before admitting defeat. I slipped through the gates to order a taxi.

I was waiting on the corner in the Friday morning drizzle when someone said my name. I turned towards the voice. The Irish boy and his friend were standing by the park gates.

'Where you going?' the Irish boy said.

'I'm going home.'

'Really?'

I hesitated, understanding the invitation in his smile. My body was heavy with exhaustion. The thought of waking up alone much worse.

It was after nine when the taxi dropped me at the boatyard. I wove up the pontoons, shoes in hand.

Back on board, I lay on the floor and stared at the ceiling, playing over the hours before with morbid fascination. *What are you doing?* I thought, before the carpet swallowed me whole.

I woke to find a blanket covering me. Felicity was sitting in the armchair next to the heater.

'Good morning,' she said.

'Morning,' I wheezed.

'Cup of tea?'

'Yes please.'

I peeled myself off the carpet. My body felt weighted, my mouth rancid with chemicals and sex. I crawled onto the chaise and lay my head on the arm.

Felicity reappeared with two mugs of tea, and we pulled the blanket over us.

'I stink,' I said.

Felicity nodded. 'It's true.'

'I'll have a bath.'

'Good night?'

'I think so.' I let out a cough that was more of a death rattle.

'Anyone I know?'

I shook my head.

'You *are* playing with a lot of fire lately.'

'I may be regressing.'

'Hmm.'

I took a sip of tea. 'Fee, is my face collapsing?'

'You just need some sleep.'

'There's no time.'

'Take a day off.'

I shook my head. 'Not an option.'

In the bathroom, I carefully painted the health back onto my face. Lately, the circles beneath my eyes had deepened to permanent grooves, my olive skin a jaundiced yellow. It was becoming less convincing in the light of day. I wriggled into a dress that was too provocative for the office and ordered my third taxi of the morning.

From the back of the air-conditioned car, I watched the gloomy city go by. The Christmas lights were up in Knightsbridge though it wasn't yet December. It was mid afternoon, the sun already setting. We drove past Hyde Park, and I saw a flash of cottage through the gates. All was quiet now, the revels of the previous night just a dream, though the wreckage of my body said otherwise. Silently, I narrated a story to keep me calm. *You're being driven to Soho in a three-hundred-pound dress. This is what being a grown-up feels like.* I took out my phone and opened Instagram to upload a photo. Hashtag: *#wednesdaynight*. I scrolled backwards through my pictures of the previous months, my life in glorious technicolour. Enviable. I breathed out slowly and sat a little straighter.

On Piccadilly, there was a nylon tent next to Green Park station near the huddled figures in their colourful sleeping bags. Many of the bags looked new, the occupants dazed at finding themselves on the street. Something was shifting in London, these displaced souls the collateral damage of change. Too easy to slip through the cracks of a city like this, where even the pavement has an undertow. I felt guilty and grateful to be safe inside the taxi with its complimentary box of tissues and smelling of Magic Tree, as it carried me towards the centre.

Climbing the stairs from the stage door, I ran through a list of possible excuses. Entering the prop cupboard, the first thing I noticed was Kristian and Archie and their weird rictus grins.

Lounging in a chair was Gabriel Grosse.

'Oh!' It fell from my lips as I froze in the doorway. He looked different from the last time I'd seen him. Puffier, his hair unkempt.

'Happy to see me?'

'Of course.' I managed to laugh. 'Welcome back.'

'Come walk with me.'

Following him downstairs, I tried to shake the feeling I'd done something wrong. The lights in the corridors burned my eyes, my temples beginning to throb.

He led me through the main space to a fire door behind the main bar that opened onto a scarlet stairwell. He stepped inside, indicating I should follow.

He lit a cigarette in the semi-dark. 'So, how are you, kid?'

'I'm . . . pretty good.' The stairwell was narrow and smelled of something chemical and damp.

'Been enjoying yourself?'

'Sure.'

He smiled. 'Fucking a lotta guys since you got here?'

My stomach flipped, a pornographic image flashing across my brain. 'No more than usual,' I said, face burning. I added, 'I guess I'm not into rich men.'

Smoke snorted from both nostrils. He was laughing.

'Figures,' he said. 'You're the artsy type. Let me guess, some lunk of an acrobat.'

I had no way of telling if he was joking, I only knew I wanted to escape the red smoking stairwell.

'A dancer,' I said and immediately regretted it.

'Nice,' he said nastily. He flicked his still-lit cigarette into the darkness below. 'So, what's on the menu today?'

I reeled off the day's schedule, trying to adjust to the new shape of my boss, while hiding my alarm. Apparently satisfied, he released me into the main room and said he'd see me later.

'Great,' I replied and when he'd gone, did something I'd never done before, and helped myself to a shot from a bottle behind the bar.

'Hi everybody, my name's Kiruna,' the woman on stage enunciated into the microphone. 'That's *Kiruna*. Not Kirsten, not Katrina, *Kiruna*.'

The bar-backs restocking the fridges and cleaners sponging the carpet around the central podium, looked up mystified.

Satisfied her message had been received, Kiruna handed me back the microphone. 'I hate it when people mispronounce my name.'

'Fair enough,' I said.

Kiruna was an actor and comedienne whom I'd first met when she'd come to live on the boat for a short stint, during which I'd learned she'd been a tap-dancing champion in her youth, a fact I'd never forgotten. Kiruna was in the lower 2.3% of the human height range, which is to say she was not much more than three feet tall, her stature belying a powerful personality that demanded both your respect and full attention.

179

'She's so adorable, I just wanna pick her up,' murmured Vinnie, a West End dancer and the Club's go-to cis male, gazing mistily at the stage.

'I wouldn't,' I said.

Vinnie already knew the routine I had in mind. There were a few moves that needed changing due to their difference in height and adjustments to handholds for certain turns, but their chemistry was undeniable. As they worked through the dance, the bar-backs and cleaners stopped what they were doing, smiles spreading across their faces.

'Too obvious,' called a voice from the back of the room.

All eyes turned to where Gabriel Grosse was watching from the bar. Now he had everyone's attention he walked over to the stage. Ignoring Vinnie and Kiruna who stared at him in confusion, he turned to me. 'Flip the script. Have *her* lift *him*.'

'Um . . .' I thought quickly. 'I guess we could *try*?'

'Just do it,' he said, irritated. 'Never go for the easy bang. We'll put it in tomorrow.'

I located Kristian on the second floor where he was regilding the golden throne. His tight-lipped expression told me he was unimpressed by Gabriel Grosse's return.

'We need to hire a flying harness and a rigger,' I said.

He looked up. 'Why?'

'Gabriel wants Kiruna to lift Vinnie.'

'But no one will be able to—'

'I know.' I sat on the floor beside him. 'But what can I do?'

Kristian frowned. 'He's not a nice man.'

'He may not stay.'

'I hope not.'

That afternoon, I tracked down a rigging contact from a travelling circus, who was in town installing the lights on Carnaby Street. He arrived in his rigger's uniform of hoodie and cargo pants. Hugging him, I caught a faint tang of wood smoke.

The winch was too slow for the stunt to work, which meant the lift had to be achieved manually, a new pulley system installed.

'What do you think?' I said once I'd shown him the room.

'We'll do our best, love,' he replied with a broad West Country grin.

Lila walked in with Beatrice. 'Still here?' she said.

'Still here.'

'Have you seen Gabriel?'

'Of course.'

'I'm so happy he's back. No offence, but he's always been my director.'

I smiled at her.

'He's taking us for dinner,' said Beatrice shyly.

Oh, be careful, little girl.

Lila linked arms with Beatrice as they moved towards the door. 'Don't work too late,' she called over her shoulder. 'You look tired.'

It was after ten before we were ready for the run-through amidst the noisy arrival of the night-time staff, the bar-backs, ushers and hostesses. By then, I'd been at the Club since midday on less than three hours' sleep.

'Does it look okay?' said Vinnie after we'd strapped him into the harness. 'It feels a bit weird.'

I tugged his vest over its bulk and stood back. 'Not too bad,' I lied. 'Let's give it a whirl.'

Vinnie took his place at the edge of the podium.

'You ready?' he said to Kiruna.

The lift had to be timed absolutely right or we risked injuring her.

'Ready,' she said.

'Okay . . . lift!' I gave a hand signal to the rigger.

Vinnie launched himself into the air and her outstretched hands, his face showing the strain of keeping his body taut as he see-sawed on top of Kiruna's strong arms.

'Well, the good news is it kind of works,' I said, looking critically at the result. 'I guess we're doing it.'

News of Gabriel Grosse's return seemed to electrify the building. Hostesses giggling in the corridors, in an extra layer of make-up – the King had returned! – newer performers asking anxiously what he'd think of their number. 'If the audience likes you, he'll like you,' I reassured them, wondering if this were true.

In the dressing room, Kiruna and Vinnie were fizzing with excitement. We'd spent the day practising the lift, Reg using the time to create a background of pale pink and blue lighting effects. Pushing doubt aside, I decided to reserve judgement until after the show.

'Do you want to get a drink before the show?' I asked Kiruna. 'You're not on till the second act.'

'Out *there*?' Kiruna's eyebrows shot up. 'No way, I'd get crushed.'

'Of course . . .' I said, trying to imagine the crowd from her perspective. I found it stressful enough fighting my way through the madness, the groping hands. It would be a nightmare for Kiruna.

'It's actually an unusually tall crowd,' she said, turning back to the mirror.

'It is?'

'Uh huh. It's the breeding, I think. All that money.'

'All those models.'

'Yup. I'll pass.'

There was no sign of Gabriel Grosse during Act One and by the intermission he still hadn't appeared. Act Two began, Athena appearing through the curtains, her endless legs whipping through the sequin fringe of her silver dress.

'Have we got something special for you tonight,' she purred. 'Who's feeling dirty out there? Let me hear you . . . Oh yeah, you guys are dirty. Give it up, for my girl *Kirstiiin* . . .'

The curtains opened to reveal Kiruna and two of the dancers, all of them dressed in grass skirts and flower crowns, swaying through Hawaiian hula to the lazy strains of the ukulele.

The audience booed and *awwed* pantomime-style as the dancers bullied Kiruna, bumping her with their hips and shunting her out the way, until they skipped from the stage, laughing bitchily, leaving her forlorn in the spotlight.

Pulling the flower crown from her head, Kiruna threw it angrily to the floor, ripping off her grass skirt to reveal the pale pink dress underneath.

At the same moment, Vinnie stepped from the wings, handsome in his black trousers and vest, the lights behind them shifting to an eighties music video dreamscape. A wave of joy rippled through the room as he bent on one knee to take Kiruna's hand and the first notes of the track began to play.

Now I've had the time of my life . . .

Lifting her arm to drape it around his neck, Vinnie trailed his fingers down Kiruna's body to take her hand. The beat kicked in and she spun out to the side, her pink skirt fanning in a circle. Then Vinnie was on his feet, and they began to dance, smiling as they moved through the beats of Johnny and Baby's iconic routine, nailing every kick, spin and dip.

By the time they paused, their lips almost touching, Vinnie on one knee, the crowd were nearly hysterical. *When people see a disabled woman, they never imagine you can dance*, said Kiruna when we first discussed the number. And it was more than that. In a space geared for 'shock' no one expected Kiruna to be the romantic lead or object of desire, no strings attached. Or rather, that *was* the punch-line: her humanity as subversive act.

Kissing Kiruna's hand, Vinnie leaped from the stage as the dancers, now clad in eighties dance wear, rejoined Kiruna to perform a call-and-response to his peacocking strut through the crowd.

Vinnie reached the podium where, after two magnificent spins, he paused to allow Archie to attach the line, as the dancers took Kiruna's arms, lifting her from the stage in one graceful move. The audience was howling now – they knew what was coming. There was only one thing needed now to bring the number home.

As the dancers bore Kiruna to the podium, I glanced over to fix my eyes on the rigger. Counting the final bars, I raised my hand to give the signal in the final moments before Vinnie launched himself into the air and disappeared.

The euphoria in the room seemed to quiver, then burst like a bubble.

I pushed my way through the crowd to the podium where

Kiruna was standing, arms by her sides. The audience looking with bemusement at Vinnie dangling like a broken
puppet, too high for her to reach. I signalled to the rigger,
who lowered him down as the show lights switched to party
mode.

'Well, that was a stupid idea.' I turned to see Gabriel
Grosse standing behind me.

Yours or mine?

I didn't say it.

'Fucking change it back.' He turned on his heel and
stalked away as the DJ dropped another track. I watched
him go, disappearing into the crowd that closed around
him, then went upstairs to collect my things.

Waiting on the corner for my taxi, my anger not yet
subsided, I considered my boss, the Mad King.

Only one end to that kind of story. Did I know it then?
Beyond a certain point all you can do is react, and cling on.
You forget to ask the question: tasked with a Mad King's
bidding, what then, does that make you?

Chapter 16

Happy: *Did he steal a kiss?*
Snow White: *He was so romantic I could not resist . . .*

The voiceover and lilting strings were interrupted by the screeching sound of a needle being dragged across a record, the girl in pigtails on the well-worn bed, looked up from her teddies in alarm.

The music changed to a sleazy R. Kelly track as a tall black man in crotch-dragging trousers came swaggering through the crowd. Grinding against the women in the audience, he filmed their laughing faces on his phone.

On stage, the girl had her hands pressed to her cheeks. Finally, her prince *had* come.

Leaping the stage in a bound, R. Kelly aimed his phone at the girl as she threw babysitter-porn poses on the bed. Eyes bulging, he bent to sniff the crotch of her frilly panties. Obediently, she whipped them off and lay back with her legs spread wide.

The number was a Gabriel Grosse original he'd requested I resurrect. The previous week he'd tasked me with another that ended with a girl firing a gun into her vagina as the lights cut to black.

Up on the bed now, R. Kelly unzipped his fly and released a long stream of fake piss down onto the girl.

All around me, people were losing their minds. Gabriel Grosse knew his audience well. Looking at their faces, lips drawn back from their teeth, my unease that had begun in the tech rehearsal guiding Reg through the beats of the number, reached fever pitch. We were doing something terribly wrong.

Shaking off the drips, R. Kelly jumped down to kneel at the foot of the bed. With a backward glance, he licked his lips and tilted back his head. Then the girl, engaging impressive Kegel muscles, pumped once, twice, shooting a perfect arc of liquid from her vagina into his open mouth.

At the side of the stage, I listened to them scream long after the curtains had shut. Turning away I almost collided with Gabriel Grosse.

'Hear that?' he shouted. 'Come meet some people.'

A group of slick-looking men were sitting at one of the VIP tables. Among them was a familiar-looking man I identified as the movie star I'd heard was one of Gabriel Grosse's close friends. Beautiful as a young man, his looks had mellowed into a sun-kissed handsomeness, though I suspected his hairline was not entirely his own.

'Wonderful,' he murmured with vacant charm.

'Director?' said a man with silver hair. 'You ought to be on stage.'

'Do you come up with all those ideas yourself?' said another.

'That's the thing about our show,' Gabriel Grosse was blathering across the table. 'The girl's always gotta come out on top.'

'I'm trying to convince your boss to let me make a documentary about him,' the silver-haired man winked. 'Perhaps you could tell me his secrets.'

I had a sudden urge to sweep their drinks from the table.

'I've got to check on a performer,' I said.

Gabriel Grosse breathed a dragon's breath of vodka fumes into my ear. 'I'm so glad you're here.'

In the strobe light faces leered as I struggled for the door, bodies staggering in the haze of dry ice, their shrieking the gibbering of the damned. Outside in the street, a December wind was blowing. It stung my cheeks, making me feel more sober than I wanted to be. Not yet ready to return to the boat where the climate on board had made the shift from 'bracing' to 'survival mode', I began to walk.

On the corner of Wardour Street, a man in a Santa hat was sitting on a piece of cardboard. 'Ho-ho-ho, god bless, ho-ho-ho, god bless,' he called to passers-by.

It began to drizzle as I crossed Leicester Square, dodging groups of slack-jawed tourists and girls handing out flyers. Somewhere in the square was the ghost of my underage-self, shivering on a corner for three pounds an hour and drink tokens. Jailbait used as club-bait. Down Piccadilly, I passed beneath bowers of shimmering lights transforming it into a golden arcade, a tired-looking doorman tipping his hat beneath the awning of the Ritz. In a doorway, someone was sleeping with a paper bag over their head. It was Christmas in London, in all its hypocrisy and splendour.

The Club would close for three days over the holiday season and reopen after Boxing Day for regulars seeking solace in a different kind of white Christmas.

Meanwhile on the boat, preparations were under way for our annual orphans' feast. Felicity and I wrapped ourselves in fur coats to peel potatoes in the kitchen, fortified by the highly flammable mulled cider Maciek kept topping up with whisky. At just after seven, we crammed the goose and as many potatoes that could fit into the boat's tiny oven, as the first guests began to arrive.

Upstairs, a dining table had been cobbled together from an old door balanced precariously on wine boxes. And if there wasn't quite enough cutlery to go round, nobody seemed to mind. For dessert, dazzled by the blue flames, we set the pudding on fire three times in a row, someone producing a bottle of liquid acid as a digestif.

Sometime after that, while the assembled guests were absorbed in recreating the Nativity using various lamps for halos, Kristian stood and gently tapped a fork against the side of his glass. The Wise Men, Mary and two sheep, stopped what they were doing.

Kristian blushed, unused to demanding attention. 'I have an announcement to make.'

'In-credible,' said Russella.

Kristian smiled before continuing. 'I've had an email from the producers of the *Rocky Horror Show* . . .'

'But why didn't they email me?' said Russella.

'. . . and they've offered me the part of Riff Raff.'

'Wonderful, bunny!' Felicity cried, amidst calls of '*Mazel tov! Bravo!*'

'When?' I asked.

'Rehearsals start in two weeks.'

'*Two weeks?*'

'I'm still waiting for their offer—'

'You have to say yes,' I said. 'Congratulations, my love.'

Later, when everyone had ventured onto the deck to set fire to the Chinese paper lanterns someone had brought, Kristian came to where I was leaning against the railings.

Attempting a smile, I burst into tears. 'I'm sorry,' I said, balling my fists into my eyes.

Kristian was already clasping me in a rare hug.

'Take me with you,' I murmured into his shoulder.

'You'll be *fine*,' he said, laughing as we released each other to watch as one by one, the lanterns began to lift like paper-bag ghosts into the inky sky. They rose into the night until a sidewind sent several of them crumpling into the dark water, another descending in an elegant spiral onto our neighbour's deck and someone had to run to put it out.

I woke the next day on top of my duvet, still wearing my fur coat. I remained motionless, gauging the extent of the damage before attempting to sit up, releasing a hacking cough like a TB sufferer. A framed poster was lying beside me, dusted with the remnants of last night's drugs and what looked like fake snow. I scraped together a puny bump, using the chemical momentum to propel me up.

'Horrors, horrors,' I muttered as I made my way along the corridor beneath the buzzing overhead light. I passed Felicity's cabin where a few stragglers were still heaped on the bed.

In the kitchen, Russella was asleep in a tangle of matted blond hair and glittery platforms. I located my phone in the pocket of my coat and ordered a taxi for twenty minutes' time. Then I staggered to the bathroom to search for my toothbrush.

The London streets were deserted as the terraces of Earl's Court gave way to the elegant townhouses of Kensington. Even Ladbroke Grove was silent as the taxi crossed the bridge over the canal.

Pulling up on the street where my parents lived, I saw the graceful plane trees had undergone their annual hobbling and stood bare and bony like mutilated hands.

Standing on the doorstep, I felt a different part of me step forward, ready to take things from here. Through the stained glass, I watched my mother's small, neat shape swim into view, her smiling face as the door swung open.

'You've launched!' she'd cried when I first told her about the Club, as if previously I'd been a rocket that had begun promisingly with fire and smoke, then toppled over.

'Happy Christmas,' I croaked, folding myself into her cashmere embrace, hoping that my hair didn't reek too much of party.

'Ooh, you smell of fags,' she said.

I stepped through the door into the hallway decorated with holly from the garden.

My father, a paper crown on his handsome bald head, appeared from the kitchen in a cloud of cooking smells.

'It's my big daughter,' he said.

'What time's lunch?' I gave him a kiss.

'Around two.'

'I'll have a quick bath then. Where's GJ?'

'Getting changed.'

'What's wrong with the bath on the boat?' my mother called as I started up the stairs.

'Pipes are frozen,' I said over my shoulder. 'GJ?' I called as I reached the landing on the second floor.

'Ah!' Her voice rang out, an exclamation in cut-glass, before she appeared in the doorway of the spare bedroom. My beautiful grandmother, in salmon-pink trousers, pearls and a bra.

'Hello, old friend,' she said as I put my arms around her, lost for a moment in her powdery smell, the softness of her ninety-five-year-old skin: tissue and velvet.

'I missed you so much,' I said.

An investigation of her affairs a few months before had revealed chaos beneath the surface: unopened post and bills unpaid. Now, in addition to the cleaner who kept her house in order, my parents had hired a second woman to help with shopping and other essential tasks.

Anxiously, I looked for signs of absence in her face, but saw only her.

'How are you, GJ?'

'Too bloody old, darling.'

'Same.'

'Ha!'

We grinned at each other, then she said, 'Darling, you look ill. You must go to bed.'

'I've probably got to do a bit of Christmas first.'

'Christmas,' said my grandmother, as if turning over this new notion in her head.

After my bath, I put on a clean dress, reapplied my make-up and went down to the kitchen. As always, it was a comfortable mess, cluttered with objects brought back from my parents' many travels, stacks of medical journals and classic motorbike magazines fighting for space with ceramic bowls of ageing fruit mixed in with biros, keys and other paraphernalia.

My father was standing at the island, uncorking a bottle of champagne. The pale gold wine fizzed from the bottle. I took a cautious sip and felt my hangover recede an inch.

'Can I do anything?' I asked.

'You could open those,' he said, nodding to a box of oysters.

I located the shucking knife and wrapped my hand in a tea towel to begin the precarious business of prising open the flaking molluscs.

'You're supposed to wait for the guests,' said my mother, coming into the kitchen.

'My lovely wife,' my father said, pouring her a glass.

My mother took it with a growl and began arranging bowls of crisps. She scrutinised me critically across the counter. 'How *is* the Club?' she said.

Tears prickled behind my eyes, and I had a desperate urge to tell her . . . what? That I was tired. More tired than I'd ever been. But then I looked at her face, so eager for good news.

'It's great, Mama,' I said.

The doorbell rang, and I swallowed the last of my champagne and poured myself another, in anticipation of the arrival of my extended family.

The dining table looked magical, trailed with real holly and ivy, silver candlesticks polished and shining against the dark green tablecloth. My grandmother, as was her habit, waited for everyone to arrive before making her entrance, leaning heavily on her stick. Still the most charming, despite everything. Now she sat at the head of the table, looking lost amidst the babble of voices. I was getting quietly drunk, sandwiched between my father and a merry male cousin, lost in memories of another Christmas, my grandmother flirting with my then boyfriend, who'd adored her.

'How's the world of burlesque?' My uncle addressed me directly over a plate of salmon.

'Fine, I hear,' I said. 'But I'm not performing anymore. I'm working for a club in Soho.'

'Soho!' my uncle said. 'I used to know it quite well. Which one?'

'The Club.'

'No, I haven't heard of it.'

'It's very cool,' said my father, and I grimaced.

'Is it? Should we come?'

'Sure,' I said. 'But the show starts at 1 a.m.'

'Ah, past my bedtime.'

I nodded sympathetically.

'Who wants pudding?' My father clapped his hands together.

The day wore on, woozy lunchtime drunkenness giving way to afternoon irritability. Excusing myself from the torment of board games, I went to lie down on the sofa. Not long after, my grandmother came in, twinkled at me, and promptly fell asleep in an armchair. Older than I'd ever seen her.

I was woken by the sound of the front door slamming, and my mother came into the living room. I uncurled myself and shuffled up to make room.

'Is everyone still here?' I muttered.

'Everyone's gone, we thought we'd let you sleep,' she said, joining me on the sofa. 'They'll be back tomorrow.'

There was a pause as I reached for the remote, a silent question that asked, *Why are you like this?* Once I'd thought it hers, but more and more, I knew that it was mine.

'Oh,' my mother said. 'Go back to Patrick Swayze.'

On the screen, Johnny and Baby were grinding in the dance studio.

'Good choice,' I said, and we settled down to watch.

We fell into a comfortable silence, lulled by the story we'd seen a hundred times before. I rested my head on my mother's shoulder.

'We made a show at the Club based on *Dirty Dancing*,' I said.

194

My mother smiled vaguely but didn't reply. For my parents so much of my life was hearsay, occurring in places they'd never see.

'It blew the roof off,' I added, pitying as I always did my sorry attempts to please.

New Year's Eve was under way. Another year and according to Mayan conspiracy theorists, another Apocalypse. All around me people were embracing, sticky lips colliding as the last pre-recorded chime rang out. Instinctively, I looked for Kristian then remembered he was gone. Someone pulled me into a hug, one of the performers, who slurred something drunk and emotional in my ear. Nearby, a hostess was atop a table, kicking bottles to the floor. Those who were not entangled waved their arms in the air and bellowed, then looked around expectantly as if waiting for something to happen. Once again, the world had failed to end. Or perhaps it had, and we were all in purgatory disguised as a Soho nightclub.

My phone vibrated crazily as message after message arrived from names I didn't recognise. They all seemed to say the same thing: *Let me in.* I turned it off.

Seeking refuge backstage, I crossed paths with Roxanne, the Club's new MC since Athena returned to the States. Long-legged and model-perfect, physically Roxanne was in the same mould as Athena but for her chirpy Essex twang. Gabriel Grosse had dealt with this by insisting she conduct her mistress-of-ceremony duties in an American accent. Essential, he said, for controlling the Club's audience of rich white boys.

'Happy New Year, love,' she said. 'You won't believe what I've just seen . . .'

In the performers' dressing room, a woman was bent backwards on the make-up counter, laughing as the Movie Star snorted cocaine off her exposed breasts, to the amusement of Gabriel Grosse, opening a bottle nearby.

Watching them, I had the sense of the world folding in on itself. The impresario and the movie star in some grotesque parody of how they were expected to behave, the revellers downstairs performing a good time.

'Who's this new girl?' the Movie Star said when he saw me there.

'You've met,' Gabriel Grosse said.

'Are you alone?' The Movie Star's eyes were glassy.

'Yes,' I said, and left.

Up on the Beach, Lavinia was sitting on the wall, her tinsel wig sparkling in the dark, smoking one of her liquorice roll-ups. Neither of us spoke, but I took the sweet brown stick she offered. We sat, our breath mingling with the smoke, beneath an icy sky that glittered here and there with the pink and green of distant fireworks.

'It's awful down there,' I said.

Lavinia chuckled softly.

'It's like everything's repeating itself. Only each time it's a little bit worse.'

'Oh luvvie,' Lavinia said. 'I'm sixty-two years old. Imagine how I feel.'

Act 3

Chapter 17

The new Soho will have more lights than ever before, neon beacons to warm the faces of those drawn to the newly minted streets. But who will come? Old Soho has slipped through the cracks, washed away down the drain with last night's piss and beer.

You've seen the original sign, dirty and broken on the roof of the Club. There's no way they'll get that husk with its sixties circuitry working again. No. The new signs will be replicas: bigger, bolder, brighter – gaudy tombstones for the glossy new mile with its hard casing of bright steel and polished glass. Soho is dead! The death-knell will toll through the wide streets of W1, echoing down Charing Cross Road to Trafalgar Square to scare away the pigeons. Let the tourists come and gape at its lovely relic, take a grinning selfie and purchase a macabre souvenir!

But not so long ago, you could still detect a heartbeat thudding deep beneath the paving stones. A well of something black and glittering, seeped through clay over decades, vibrating with the malevolent life force of a thing who knows its time has come, but won't give up without first sinking in its teeth for the final thrashing fight.

The pirates came on the morning tide, not long after sunrise. The crew and I were in the kitchen, twitchy with anticipation as we made a second round of coffee.

In the past, the boat had been dragged onto the tidal mudflats for repairs to her rusted hull, but the boatyard was under new management who'd requested all vessels provide certificates attesting to their river-worthiness, and so we were off to dry dock in the western reaches of the city.

The pirates' ship was an oil-stained tug with a stuttering pit bull of an engine. On deck stood an unsmiling man and a hyperactive youth who was stripped to the waist despite the icy morning.

A third man hidden inside the wheelhouse, backed the tug towards the boat, the youth hopping across the gap to secure heavy towropes, casting wary glances at Maciek watching from the prow, in sunglasses and amorphous black like a fashion-forward crow.

'Look, Mum, gypsy trade,' Maciek murmured.

'Hush you,' I said.

The electricity and water were disconnected and the ropes tethering us to land untied. Felicity and I squealed as the boat began to drift from the pontoon towards open water.

'The roof!' I cried, hauling myself up.

On Battersea Bridge a few people stopped to watch. Someone waved and I waved back. Behind them, Albert Bridge rose like a castle in the early morning mist. These familiar views swung past in a slow curve as the boat rocked and trembled, buffeted by the turbulent river currents, and I had a vision of us capsizing, the boat and everything on it dragged to the riverbed to bewilder future divers seeking to explore the wreck. What would they make of the flamingo, the bullet holes, and costumes rotted away to moss?

Having completed our turn, the strong little tug revved its engine, the boat surging forwards as we set a course for the west.

The journey would take two hours. Our excitement subsiding only as the towers of Wandsworth gave way to the leafier views of Putney, and we settled on the roof to watch London go by.

'Kristian would've loved this,' I said softly, as we passed around a hip flask to keep warm. Lulled by the gentle rocking, we slipped into contented silence.

From the water you could sense how the city had grown, country villages swallowed, market roads becoming thoroughfares, the World's End once the outskirts of civilisation, if civilised is what cities are. Down on the river, history and time are layered like sediment, but ask any mudlarker and they'll tell you that a clay pipe is just a Georgian fag butt. That things never really change.

Beyond the riverside pubs and rowing clubs of Richmond, Eel Pie Island crouched in the river like the Lost Boys' Neverland hideaway. Buried in greenery along the banks, nestled small wooden dwellings connected by rickety boardwalks leading up from the water, where all manner of river craft bobbed next to makeshift moorings. The tug's engine puttered now as we drifted slowly through this strange new kingdom.

At the boatyard, the pirates called to each other in curt barks, scrambling to secure the boat to the dock. We climbed down from the roof and stood uncertainly on deck, dazed at having arrived.

'Look.' Felicity pointed to where the river was creeping over the footpath.

'Mind yer feet,' said the youth, who sprinted from the dock, dodging sure-footed around the growing puddles of the incoming tide.

'We'd better get a move on,' I said.

We went back inside and quickly gathered our belongings. Suitcases in tow, we slopped our way through two inches of water towards the bridge that would take us to dry land. Glancing back at the boat, I was moved to see how small and shabby she looked away from her Chelsea home.

At the nearest station, the crew split up, Maciek bound for the Kensington penthouse of a Hong Kong millionaire, and Felicity to Brighton. I would return to Soho to stay at the apartment where the Club housed visiting performers. I tried to quell my uneasiness on the train back to town with thoughts of central heating, but the image of the boat's empty mooring unsettled me, like the gap in a familiar smile.

The performers' apartment was a grim affair, grubby and white, with utilitarian bedrooms and much-used beds. Putting my bag down in one of the rooms, I sat gingerly on the edge of the mattress. Located on the third floor of a grotty building round the corner from the Club, it had former brothel written all over it. Some of the performers said it was haunted, and I wouldn't have been surprised. Its anonymity reminded me of Magda's hostel, the same sad stories sunk into the walls.

I went to investigate the facilities and found Yozmit in the kitchen, a headliner from New York whose numbers were part-sculpture, part-ritual. Long black hair and a beautiful ageless face with features halfway between male and female, she made room at the counter where she was engaged in the task of cooking noodles over a hotplate.

'Hungry?' she offered.

I shook my head. The excitement of the day had killed my appetite and I couldn't yet face a conversation. Yozmit tipped the noodles into a bowl, nodded once, and took it with her to her room.

I stood in the kitchen under the violent strip lights, thinking about the boat. A fortnight wasn't long, but being without my home made me anxious in a way I couldn't articulate. I thought about calling Magda but I was too weary, my soul stretched too thin.

I went to my bedroom and lay down. Directly above me, the ceiling had been repaired in a shape that was almost human. Rose had told me of the night she'd woken up screaming. She'd looked down to discover her body covered in rubble and plaster, a cinder block on her pillow where her head had been. Was it my turn tonight? I rolled over in my clothes and turned out the light.

It was early when I woke, startled from my anxious dreams by shouting in the street. Groggily, I kicked off the duvet, receiving a mild electric shock. After a lukewarm shower, I pulled on yesterday's clothes. Yozmit's bedroom door was open and I could see her, eyes closed in meditation, cross-legged on the bed.

Closing the front door softly behind me, I went out to search for breakfast.

It was the dullest of February days, the streets soggy and mean. I chose a greasy spoon that served fry-ups and microwaved baked potatoes and sat in the window. Looking at the menu I saw they offered a glass of milk for 50p, and ordered one along with a bacon sandwich. The milk arrived, pale and weirdly blue, tasting vaguely of chlorine. Outside, daytime workers scurried by in the drizzle. It had been a long time since I'd found myself among people with scrubbed morning faces. It was easy to forget there was more than one London.

The thought of returning to the performers' apartment was depressing, so I wandered along Oxford Street, drifting in and out of shops that were just opening their doors. I bought new lingerie without trying it on and a pair of boots I didn't need; red lipstick and a concealer that promised miracles.

I found my feet leading me down familiar rat-runs towards the Club, at least beneath the pavement there was no grim morning. On Old Compton Street, a parade of fifty-odd people in funeral finery were walking in slow procession behind a cardboard coffin. Some of them carried wreaths, others' signs reading: *SOS, Save Our Soho, Save Madame JoJos*. I watched them go by, following a little way behind, torn between knowing that surely this was where my loyalties lay, embarrassed at how we must appear to those at whom the protest was aimed. Our non-existent power.

Once, at the Club, I'd laughed in the face of a Suit who, referring to the prime minister, commented, 'Our boy's doing a good job, isn't he?' Angry at being mocked, he'd hissed, 'You people. You don't even know what the G8 is.' And he was right. I'd gone home and googled it, should it ever come up again. People like me, people like us, the ones on the fringes, looking down our noses at people like him. I hadn't realised they despised us back.

The funeral moved on towards Brewer Street where the wreaths were laid at the boarded-up front of Soho's oldest drag club. I continued to the Club's stage door, entertaining gloomy thoughts of the world.

'So, talk me through it,' I said, surveying the costume covering the stage, a vast gown patterned with blue and white figures like a *toile* from the eighteenth century, only when you looked closer, the images were Yozmit herself.

Yozmit closed her eyes. 'At the beginning, there is only a sea of energy.'

'Your skirt?'

'Yes, my skirt.'

I was learning that discussing Yozmit's technical requirements was to be in the presence of a shaman; you had to divine the meaning in the signs.

'Slowly, the bubbles of reality begin to appear.'

The bubbles were four dancers, hidden beneath the skirt with only their heads visible beneath transparent domes. They would stand at four corners of the stage with Yozmit in the centre as a living totem.

Yozmit demonstrated. 'They start to rise and fall like this as the spaceship gathers power . . .'

We were interrupted by a scream from the stairwell and one of the cleaners appeared in the room, her eyes white with panic.

'There's a dead man,' she said. 'Downstairs.'

'Where?' I said.

'In the toilet.'

I looked at Archie. 'We should check.'

'What's happening?' asked Yozmit.

'We're coming back,' I called over my shoulder as we hurried from the room.

'Do you think it's real?' said Archie as we took the stairs two at a time.

'We'll find out.'

The disabled toilet was accessed through the lobby and was used mainly by staff as an illicit cocaine pitstop. Approaching it, I saw the door was slightly ajar.

Archie stepped forward, put a hand on it and pushed. It opened a few inches, blocked by a heavy object on the other side. 'Oh god.'

I put my shoulder to the door and the gap grew wider. Peering in, I saw a large man slumped face down next to the toilet. On closer inspection, I could see the fabric of his suit moving with the rise and fall of the man's broad back.

'He's not dead,' I said. 'Come on, help me shift him.'

Archie added his weight and together we managed to wedge the door wider.

'Hey.' I poked the man's leg with the toe of my shoe. 'Wake up.'

He let out a low moan, stirred, a large hand reaching out to grasp the rim of the toilet. 'Fucking pissed,' he muttered.

The man pulled himself to a seated position and stared at us through bloodshot eyes. 'The fuck am I?'

'You're at the Club,' I said. 'But it's probably time you went home.'

Outside we watched him weaving down the alley in the direction of Shaftesbury Avenue, then went back to the lobby where we collapsed in howls of laughter.

'His eyes,' Archie gasped, doubled over on the golden gun. 'How do you pass out for that long? It's crazy.'

'He probably picked up the wrong drink.'

'Date-rape drugs?'

Archie stopped laughing.

'It happens,' he said. 'More than you'd think.'

'Really?'

'It happened to me.'

I gaped.

'It wasn't too bad. I started feeling weird and managed to get backstage.'

'That's horrible.'

Archie shrugged. 'Come on, let's put the cleaner out of her misery.'

The cleaner looked at us with wounded eyes when we explained with barely suppressed giggles that the corpse had been a drunken man. Then the dancers began to arrive, and we had to tell the story again, Archie and I taking it in turns to mimic the man's zombie-stagger.

When everyone stopped laughing, I saw the cleaner had gone.

I spent the week in a state of limbo. I'd wake, always too early, in the performers' apartment, my heart racing before I remembered where I was. I'd take my melancholic walks through Soho, my feet leading me aimlessly in circuits through the narrow streets, before descending once more to the Club where I'd remain until after the show had finished. The highlight of my days were my conversations with Yozmit whose peaceful presence diffused the Club's toxic stickiness, like an emissary from a kinder universe. Articulate and deeply thoughtful, she told me stories of arriving as a teenager in the US from South Korea, a place where homosexuality and gender identity were so taboo that the first time she'd heard either mentioned was during a school psychology lesson, when the class was informed that homosexual and transgender individuals were mentally sick, requiring hospital treatment. She told me of her misadventures as a K-Pop star, locked in a studio and beaten by her management for being unapologetically feminine; later a fashion career in LA, all of which led finally to the birth of 'Yozmit' in the early days of the Club. For Yozmit, stage persona and performance were a spiritual practice of self-realisation, and medicine for the stricken soul.

'Mundane as it sounds,' she said, as we sat eating bibim-bap in a restaurant around the corner from the Club, 'we become whole only by understanding and embodying our dark side. Our dark psyche.'

'But do you have one?' I smiled.

'Of course! As a man – a Korean feminine man – I'm disempowered. Bottom of the caste system. I created Yozmit as my higher power goddess alter ego, balancing the sacred masculine and feminine within me. An empowered being from this disempowered body.'

'And the Club?' I asked. 'Was that part of embodying your dark side?'

'Oh sure. The Club is a dark gate. But sometimes it's necessary to pass through those. That isn't to say it's bad; everything has two sides. It's the dualistic nature of the world we live in.'

I thought of Rose and the stories she told while brutalising her own body, of Fancy taking flight in nothing but the skin she was born in. Of hatching from the egg and singing my pledge for freedom night after night. There was a through-line connecting all of us, a kind of alchemy we were reaching for to transcend the narratives we'd been handed, in exchange for one we'd chosen for ourselves.

Yozmit's Spaceship closed the show that week, her skirt billowing like a parachute over the audience. Once the spaceship had landed safely on stage, the tall headpiece covering her face was removed ready for her *transmission* that Yozmit, trained in the art of traditional Korean opera, would sing, imparting the goddess's message of self-acceptance, a gospel of transformation, before inviting the audience beneath her skirt to their portal of the unknown . . . *In this way we are reminded that we are all star-seed.*

Watching from the sidelines, I was amazed to see the

audience dancing like children, their faces open and laughing as their hands stretched to touch the surface of the fabric. Gabriel Grosse was wrong. Offered cruelty and they behaved accordingly but given an alternative they opened to the possibility of wonder.

Abandoning my watcher's post, I ducked beneath the skirt and raised my arms. Stiff fabric rasped against my palms, and I experienced a flicker of excitement. I turned my face to the sky, closed my eyes and began to dance, eddies of energy swirling about me, and for a moment I was transported to more innocent dance floors where smiling strangers embraced, lost in music and dreams of different future, where there was no Club, no Gabriel Grosse, wounded boat, heart, or city . . .

The music ended.

The stagehands came to carry the skirt back to the stage, those who'd been dancing left blinking on the dance floor, unsure of what had happened. The spaceship a pile of crumpled fabric once more, the Club just a club, star-seed only drunks.

A week passed with still no word from the pirates, so I called the number of the dry dock. It rang for a long time before someone answered and I recognised the voice of the unsmiling man.

'Bad news I'm afraid,' he said, and the back of my neck went cold.

'Hull's rusted through in places,' he continued. 'Someone had the bright idea of patching her with concrete.'

'Okay. But can you fix her?'

'It'll cost you forty.'

'Forty?'

'Forty thousand.'

'I don't have forty thousand pounds,' I managed.

'We could patch her up for twenty. But I can't guarantee you won't have to do it again in a few years' time.'

'I haven't got twenty.'

'You're in a bit of a pickle then, love.'

When we hung up, I tried to access an emotional response but found none. Or it was so great I could not gauge its shape. Panic, I thought. Cry. My eyes homed in on an oily handprint on the wall next to my bed. Lube, perhaps.

I thought of all the times when crossing the frosted deck to pump the water from the bilge, had proved too much to contemplate. Entire winters gone by. Like so many things I'd neglected, I'd pushed my captain's responsibilities aside. Sometimes it was enough just trying to live.

In a previous life, the boat was one of the fastest vessels of her day. Built for speed, long and dart-like, motor torpedo boats had to fire both rounds simultaneously or risked going into a spin. When I first found her, she'd been the property of a retired captain of the Royal Marines, who'd converted her himself in the sixties. He'd chosen me as the boat's caretaker after I wandered on board having seen an ad on the internet, offering me a deal of interest-free monthly instalments, until I'd paid him back in full. I'd tried to honour his generosity by preserving the boat's spirit, loving her fiercely in my haphazard way. But I had not taken care of her. In the seven years I'd lived onboard she'd physically declined despite all my attempts to redecorate. And now I was responsible for what even a world war had not been able to achieve. My boat was sinking, and there was nothing to be done.

It was a different vessel that returned to the moorings, smaller somehow and derelict, as if it had been only our belief keeping her afloat. The crew and I stood on the pontoon as she was backed into her berth, like mourners watching a coffin. The boatyard had given us six months' grace.

The gangplank in place, we sat in the living room cradling mugs of whisky.

'Bastards,' said Felicity.

For once even Maciek's nihilism seemed to fail him.

None of us had considered the boat might not pass her survey. She'd always been a place of magic, a sanctuary just to the left of reality. But now reality had come for us and soon we'd be adrift in a world we did not fully comprehend nor trust.

And we were not the only ones in trouble. An investment brochure had been circulated, showing designs for a new fleet of luxury yachts scheduled to take the place of the old houseboats. The boatyard, it turned out, was one of the last stretches of undeveloped real estate in central London.

The shell-shocked boat owners met to discuss whether there was anything to be done, but looking at those gathered around the pub table I knew we were fucked. Kindly people with worried faces, some oil-stained, a little eccentric, rocking moth-eaten woollens. A dog wearing a bandana. Hopeful talk about an online petition. In other words, *prey*. There was no place for our community in the city's new skyline. It would be like holding back the tide.

Chapter 18

What is a captain without a ship, a showgirl without a show? The stories we tell about ourselves are key to our survival. Who is it you think you are? Perhaps you are a tailored suit, a Coutts account, or a modern-day P.T. Barnum or Kray? A rebel marching to the beat of your own drum. And would any of this matter if there was no one looking on?

Time to consider now what it is you require. Comedy, tragedy, or cautionary tale? The ending not yet clear. What flavour of resolution would satisfy; to see her fall and how far? Recall that in cabaret the normal rules do not apply, I'd suggest what's needed now is a Closer. A big fucking bang. Something to make you stay – and pay – to spin that wheel of possibility only the night can bring.

After the boat's return from the Island, life at the Club took on the quality of a dream, days blurring into one long rehearsal and longer night. There was no time to grieve and I was glad of it, and if what inspiration I'd once possessed had been reduced to a small trickle, well, it would return. There was no other choice.

'I don't like it,' Calypso said.

'Baked beans aren't exactly sexy,' said Charlie the doorman. 'And she's fat.'

'Actually, she isn't,' I said.

'Feedback from my clients was that she was really quite fat,' said Calypso.

This was not the first time there'd been complaints about the installations in the VIP; seven sins staged over seven weeks. Easy to create, my intention was they'd give me time to breathe.

For Sloth, we'd created a hoarder's living room heaped with trash and fast-food containers, with an exquisite doll-like performer slumped in front of an old TV where porn played on the jumping screen. The following week, three naked girls in Bettie Page wigs and rubber skull masks, played poker around a table. On the third, a buxom Diana Dors lookalike romped across a table laden with a variety of messy foods. But Gluttony had proved too much for managers to stomach.

'What does Gabriel think?' I said.

The managers either side of the empty seat where Gabriel Grosse never sat, looked uncomfortable.

The accountant cleared his throat. 'The installations aren't on-brand,' he said. 'We're known for being sexy.'

'Sexy like Rose's toilet show?' I said.

A dozen pairs of sleep-bruised eyes bored into me.

'Or a girl firing a gun into her vagina?'

The accountant frowned. 'It's a question of bodies. Some bodies are more appropriate than others.'

'How about something immersive?' said Calypso.

'The installations are immersive,' I said.

'Something glamorous, high-end.' She ignored me.

'Agreed,' said Charlie. 'High-end is what we need.'

They were beginning to circle, sharks attracted by the scent of blood.

'I'll speak to Gabriel,' I said. 'If he doesn't like it, we'll pull it.'

I looked around the table, daring them to argue. I might be a depleted force but I still had the boss's ear. None of them, I noticed, looked particularly convinced.

There was a missing tooth in Rose's smile as she enveloped me in one of her wonderful hugs.

'I'd forgotten it was today,' I said, my body limp with relief as she pressed me against her breasts. Thrown by the light-brown wig, I hadn't recognised the figure on the stage surrounded by open suitcases.

'I've been missing you all.' She released me.

'A lot's been happening.'

She showed the gap again, and I wondered how much she knew.

'What's all this?' I said, turning my attention to the contents of the suitcases.

'Just a little something for fashion week. *The Devil Wears Prada*?'

'Anna Wintour?'

'The High Priestess herself,' Rose twinkled. 'Well, what's the holy book of that world? Now imagine the ultimate act of worship.'

I was imagining hard, when an angry-looking woman came striding into the room accompanied by Calypso.

It's Mary Lamb, I thought.

'Christ, this place stinks,' she announced. 'What a fucking shithole.'

Calypso laughed then stopped abruptly in the laser-beam of the woman's glare. Mary Lamb was a legend in certain circles, a media figure with a St Tropez-glaze, she had a reputation for being vile.

Calypso noticed us watching, panic flashing across her

face. Mary Lamb, who didn't miss a trick, whipped her head in the direction of the stage.

'Hello,' I said.

'This is our director,' said Calypso, her eyes pleading with mine. 'And Rose, one of our star performers.'

Mary Lamb scowled. 'I've seen you,' she said to Rose. 'You're fucking hilarious.'

'That's very kind,' said Rose.

'Rose is one of our star-turns,' said Calypso.

Mary Lamb ignored her. 'You're the director?' she said to me.

'Yes.'

'The show's the best thing about this dump.'

'Thank you.'

'For some unknown reason I've decided to have my party here, so I'll be talking to you.'

'Sure thing,' I said, smiling a warning for Calypso's benefit.

After they'd gone, Rose and I went out to the 24-hour diner on Old Compton Street, where I ordered enough food to keep me going through the evening.

When Rose asked for hot water with lemon, I saw she was leaner than before.

'You're not hungry?' I asked.

'I'm on a special diet,' she said. 'Just beef and eggs, very simple.'

She described a new number for which she'd taught herself to shit on command. It involved Rose eating strawberries dipped in her own faeces; dark political satire on phoney government promises, the tax breaks and other incentives that were nothing more than a dirty trick.

215

'But was it hard?' I asked. 'The first time?'

She shook her head. 'Not at all.'

A waiter arrived with a plate of falafels and placed it on the table between us. We eyed them in silence. I knew other performers who injured themselves on stage in the name of entertainment, who swallowed live neon tubes or swung from hooks in the flesh of their back. But Rose was going further than anyone I'd heard of. And though I wanted to ask, 'Where does this end?', there was nothing unconsidered in Rose's numbers, or the violence she put her body through. Her life and her work were one and the same, dedicated to the living stories she told on stage, night after night. An ascetic existence as disciplined as any athlete or spiritual devotee.

'I suppose,' I said. 'It's already been inside you.'

'Exactly,' said Rose.

'But do they deserve it?' I blurted.

'Do who?'

'The audience. The people at the Club.'

Rose smiled patiently, to my amazement her voice cracked as she explained: 'You know, Ruby . . . Our clientele, they're upper echelon. Economically speaking. But they're surrounded by people who aren't genuine with them, who want things from them. All the sedatives of life are right at their fingertips so they can insulate themselves from being actual human beings. And so, what they really need is to feel. They need very badly to feel.'

We walked back towards the Club and Rose stopped at a newsagent to purchase a copy of *Vogue*. People stared at her less in Soho, perhaps used to seeing different kinds of people, or it could have been the wig. Rose was female-presenting now, with plans for facial feminisation surgery.

I wondered how much it would cost and how long she'd been saving.

The rest of the afternoon dragged on, with a string of failed auditions, culminating in a magician whose chicken escaped, running in circles around the room. In rehearsals, the dancers were in a mutinous mood, stroppy and uncooperative, unwilling to go through the numbers they'd done a hundred times before.

'But what's the *point*?' Kitty complained.

'You're getting paid,' I snapped back.

A rat's nest in my inbox, bullshit and bickering. One from a performer friend I'd auditioned the previous week who I'd had to inform would never work at the Club.

An hour before doors, I was prone on the prop cupboard sofa. My body felt weighted, but sleep wouldn't come, I was too wired, my neck stiff with adrenalin. The only thing that worked these days was the Valium I'd sweet-talked my GP into giving me. Sometimes living in Chelsea did have its uses.

'What are you doing?'

I opened my eyes to Archie standing above me.

'Sleeping,' I said.

'There are better places.'

I closed my eyes again.

'The accountant spoke to me,' Archie said. 'About the installations.'

'You know what I'm done with? Everyone's opinion.'

'You're not helping by being stubborn.'

'They're gunning for me. It doesn't matter what I do.'

'Suit yourself.' Archie picked up his iPad.

I rolled on my front and mumbled into my arms.

'What did you say?'

I lifted my head. 'I said, I miss Kristian.'

Archie raised an eyebrow, then sighed. 'So do I.'

I sat up and rubbed my eyes with both hands, and out of habit, checked my emails on my phone. At the top of the list was one from Calypso, announcing her hiring of a pair of showgirls as resident performers for the VIP. What was Calypso doing hiring performers?

Anger surged through me and before I knew it I'd bashed out a response, sent cc-all.

I've seen these showgirls before, and they are awful. *The last time, the table they were performing on collapsed and it was the worst part of the show.*

As soon as I sent it, I felt uneasy. I checked the list of email addresses in Calypso's announcement and recognised the performers' names. My stomach plummeted. Then my phone rang, Calypso's name on the screen. 'What the actual *fuck?*'

By the time we hung up, one of the showgirls had replied, a dignified response. I immediately wrote back apologising, citing stress. I told her the truth, that I was utterly ashamed, but the damage had been done.

Message sent, I looked up from my phone. Exhaled.

Archie was watching me from across the room. 'It doesn't suit you, you know.'

'What doesn't?'

'Being a bitch.'

That night I drank my way through the whiskies on the top shelf of the VIP.

'Give me something I haven't tried,' I said to Enzo, who looked unimpressed.

'You've tried everything.'

'So, let's start at the beginning.' Occasionally we still attempted a desultory flirt but our banter had a hollow ring.

He slid over twenty quid's worth of something golden and peaty. I raised the glass and drained it and went to watch Rose close the show. As I descended, the cacophony from below told me she'd already started.

I reached the front just as the curtains were closing on Rose bent-double, forcing torn pages from the world's greatest fashion magazine inside her. The baying of the crowd was deafening. *A ritual and a prayer.* Those were the words she'd used to describe the number. Embedded within it was its true meaning; Rose's response to the powers who use a holy book as an excuse to torture and murder gay men and people like her.

I slipped behind the side of the curtain. On stage, Rose was leaning over the toilet cistern as Archie and another stagehand moved forward to begin the clean-up. Slowly, she straightened and removed the handle of the plunger she'd been using to ram the pages inside her.

Rose had told me that with enough preparation her numbers were no longer painful – not exactly – but sometimes her body was left in a state of shock. I watched her make her way unsteadily to the back of the stage, as if unsure of where she was.

On the other side of the curtain, the crowd continued to scream for more.

Outside, Soho was screaming too. Stepping from the stage door I was forced from the pavement by a gang of drunks walking shoulder to shoulder. A rickshaw driver swore as I cut across his path, and I stepped between two parked cars to protect myself. *I'm invisible.* It came to me in a flash like the first step towards madness. Around me the lights swirled and bled together. Home. It was the only thought that remained. Sleep. Try not to dream.

I woke the next day with icy cheeks, a feeling of heaviness in my limbs. Curled in the warm pocket of my bed, I willed myself to get up and found that I couldn't. I sent a brief text to Archie letting him know I was ill, then turned my phone off, immediately slipping into unconsciousness.

It was night when, finally, I shuffled from my cabin. In the kitchen, I made a saucepan of pasta and took it upstairs to eat in front of the electric heater. The room was gloomy, lit by a single lamp, the other bulbs in the room fallen prey to the boat's ancient circuitry. Kristian had always replaced them when they blew. How long had we been living in darkness? My ears were ringing with tinnitus, a hangover from the Club's sound system that never completely left. I finished the pasta and went back to bed.

I slept through the following day, waking only to use the bathroom. In the corridor, I heard Felicity and Maciek's cabin doors sliding open and closed, the toilet flushing on the other side of the wall. From the depths of my fever, my bed seemed to rise and fall with the tide.

The next time I woke, sun was streaming through my skylight. I blinked through gritty eyelids in the unfamiliar brightness.

Uncertain on my feet, I made my way along the corridor towards the smell of coffee and something being fried. At the stove, Felicity was manning a pan, Maciek perched on a stool at the counter.

'She lives,' Felicity said.

'What day is it?'

'Sunday, poppet. Want some omelette? Smoked salmon, mascarpone, and tears,' she waved the pan in my direction.

'Tears?' I took a seat next to Maciek.

'For the Last Brunch.'

I frowned, not understanding. Then I remembered. 'It's not tomorrow?' I turned to Maciek.

'I like your state,' he said.

Maciek was leaving. Bound for Beijing and a job as creative director of a Chinese fashion brand. How he'd manifested this situation as much a mystery as everything else about him. Had I known? I supposed I had, but like so much else it had been swallowed by the Club.

'I'm sorry, cabin boy,' I said, 'I've been distracted.'

'Yes,' said Felicity. 'But you're here now.'

After we'd eaten, we bundled up in woolly hats and scarfs and walked along the Embankment towards the bridge. There was a brisk breeze over the river, sheets of light shining on the surface of the dark water.

Walking through the park where early crocuses were poking their tips through the mud, I started to feel dizzy, and we found a bench where I could sit down.

'I feel a hundred years old,' I said.

'You don't look a day over ninety.' Felicity linked her arm through mine.

The car boot sale in the school playground had once been our regular Sunday haunt, much of the boat furnished with its booty, purchased for pennies, and carried back like treasure. We bought polystyrene cups of sugary tea at a burger van and joined the crowd rummaging among the tables of bric-a-brac. At one stall an old woman, her twiglet-fingers groping ceramic figurines, was joking with a vast man, a tiny dog tucked under his arm. Further up, a woman in a sculptural headscarf haggled good-naturedly with a hungover fashion student and I felt a sudden wild affection for the car boot sale and its patrons. The sanity in these small exchanges.

While Maciek was examining a pocket-sized book on raw food, Felicity and I pooled our resources to purchase a child-sized doll missing the back of its head, which we presented to him as a farewell gift. Maciek put it astride his shoulders for the walk home beneath the stares of families out for an afternoon stroll. The Bird Lady was sitting on her bench when we arrived at the moorings. I thought I saw the shadow of a smile when she saw us with the doll.

On board, we opened a bottle of wine while Maciek threw clothes into a vast suitcase and tipped them out again, Felicity and I trying on items of bizarre fashion to parade around the room.

At around midnight, Felicity wobbled to her cabin, and I lay on the floor, flicking idly through a translation of the Koran, Maciek's choice of airport read, he said, because it discouraged people from sitting next to him.

From my front, I could see specks of glitter and ancient tobacco embedded in the threadbare carpet, and a wave of red-wine wooziness came over me.

'Bedtime I think,' I said. 'What time are you leaving, cabin boy?'

He told me nine o'clock which I knew was a lie and that Maciek was bad at goodbyes, but said I'd see him in the morning. Before going down, I cast a final glance at one of the most fascinating creatures I'd encountered and went to bed without setting my alarm.

Chapter 19

The care home was an ugly place, utilitarian in the way all hospitals are, brick too red, lines too straight, sliding doors and linoleum and the smell of stale food. My parents had chosen it because it had a reputation for good care.

I took the train to the small town by the river, bracing myself for heartbreak. I'd known the day was coming but hadn't expected it so soon.

After registering at the reception, I followed the halls to the dementia ward, listening to the strange sounds coming from the numbered rooms to either side, avoiding lost-looking souls in the corridor and communal sitting room, where one old man crawled on hands and knees.

Inside a small room containing a hospital bed and basic furniture, my grandmother was drinking tea from a heavy porcelain mug with a chocolate logo on the side. My mother told me she'd thrown one at a nurse and been threatened with plastic should she ever do it again. 'That *won't* be necessary,' my grandmother had replied with characteristic hauteur. I'd been horrified by the story, at the thought of her living under somebody else's rules with penalties for bad behaviour; free will and dignity being so inextricably tied.

'Yummy, yummy!' my grandmother cried when she saw me and opened her arms wide.

I sat in the chair next to her, my eyes straying to the photographs selected to arrange about the room, the ornaments and few soft furnishings to make it feel like 'home'.

I tried to make small talk, avoiding the fact of where we were, my grandmother drifting in and out of conversation, her voice trailing as her eyes grew distant, the edges of her consciousness like so many open threads. I had the sensation of being lost in time, part of me back in the drawing room of her former house, where I'd escape for weekends when life got too much. Her own accomplished watercolours on the walls, paper weights catching the light, seashells, potpourri, Campari soda on ice. Evenings spent talking, me greedy for her stories.

At one stage, a frowning woman in a grey dress appeared in the doorway. 'You. You stole my handbag,' she accused my grandmother.

'You get out!' my grandmother told her sternly. 'My granddaughter is here,' before a nurse came to lead the woman away.

I'm sorry, I wanted to tell her. I'm sorry you're here. That I'm not enough of a grown-up to find another way. But I could not say it, so asked the nurse for two more cups of tea, and kept my grief secret until it was time to leave, stumbling tear-blind through the sliding doors to the world outside.

Felicity left for Brighton in January, the last of the crew to leave. It was a melancholic parting. 'Be careful, bunny,' she told me before she went.

'Always,' I said as I watched her wheel her suitcase down the gangway.

Alone on the boat I could not bear its silence, so avoided going back unless it was to sleep. Lock-ins, after-parties, chasing fun that never quite happened, waking sometimes in unfamiliar beds in distant parts of London and heading straight to work where I kept an extra make-up bag and clean underwear. It was not great sex, there was no dance, no story. Something to convince myself I existed outside the Club.

One morning, I awoke to find myself in a shipping container on a traveller site beneath the Westway flyover. I opened one gluey eye then the other, saw empty bottles, the contents of an ashtray spilled across the floor. Next to me a body stirred, the girl's slender arm thrown across me, curly hair obscuring her face. Later, we went for breakfast at a greasy spoon around the corner, where we drank tea and held hands before I called a taxi. On my way to the Club, I found that I was weeping, her touch the kindest thing that had happened in months.

Life continued in this way, rising heavy with Valium, returning to Soho like an automaton that knows only one track, moments registering like postcards arriving from faraway lands. I'd find myself involved in scenes – for they had the cardboard staginess of a play – unsure of how I got there, once coming to in the boardroom in the company of Calypso and two women earnestly discussing the contents of a flight case of luxury sex toys.

'What are your thoughts?' one of the women addressed me.

'I completely agree,' I said.

January, February, underwater, underground. Swimming in a twilight world like the depths of the ocean. Out on the floor, I was hustling – or trying to. Making circuits of the Club, searching for opportunities, a place to jump. I met so many men. Boring men, arrogant men, men in suits, men who worked in music, TV, money and film. They all had one thing in common: they didn't care about the show or my part in it, though happy to flatter my ego if it meant getting me into bed, turning spiteful when they realised it wouldn't happen. I'd been mistaken. Just as my career in cabaret had ended in a cul-de-sac, the Club led to nothing but itself.

It was a bitter March, colder even than the previous winter months. Somewhere I must have seen a card, or a deal on flowers, because I resolved to visit my grandmother on Mother's Day. But when the day arrived and I woke hungover after a long stint at the Club, the thought of the home filled me with such bleakness I could not face it. Next week, I told myself. I'd see her next week. And besides, she wouldn't know it was Mother's Day.

But I did not go the following Sunday because three days after that, my grandmother swung for the old woman who'd accused her of stealing one too many times, and fell.

Something left my body when my mother gave me the news, a ghost piloting me through the motions of telling Archie what had happened, leaving the Club to travel to my grandmother's bedside.

My parents were already there when I arrived. In the darkened room, the curtains drawn, a woman who in some ways resembled my grandmother was lying in the bed, her hands like balls of white bandage.

I sat next to her and touched the softness of her arm above the bandage, stroked it.

'GJ, it's me,' I said, but couldn't tell if she was there.

For two days, we stayed in the room, my mother applying Vaseline to my grandmother's lips with a cotton bud as her breathing grew slow and ragged. When the nurses came to change her, I took walks around the town, down to the river, once stopping in a branch of Space NK to spend fifty pounds on a rose-scented candle that I brought back to her room to perfume it.

In the hushed dark, I watched her grow smaller, waiting for death a strangely peaceful thing. Time suspended, quiet like you've never known,

We ate our lunch in the common room, where we were approached by two little women arm in arm, one of them with extravagant hairs on her chin. Cheerfully, they told us about their trip to town that morning, what they'd seen and done, happy in their shared fantasy. The old man on all-fours crawled over and enquired, *did we have a biscuit?*

'We have cake,' I offered, and he accepted a slice. The sight of lemon drizzle caused a ripple among the residents, more of them drifted over and we found ourselves hosting a surreal tea party, where the guests spoke in mumbles and broken sentences, others who did not speak at all, each lost in their own mysterious dream.

After our second night of sleeping in chairs, my mother told me gently that the dying will sometimes hold on when their family is near. The ghost inside me nodded, understanding, and made plans to go back to London.

I returned to the Club on the Monday, not knowing what else to do.

I was in tech rehearsals for Mary Lamb's party when I received the call.

At the back of the darkened auditorium, I stood unseeing. On stage, the lights rotated blindly as the dancers went through the motions. The music started and stopped. I waited for the blow but there was only a numbness. A low roaring sound. A landscape of loss too vast to perceive.

I went back to my seat in front of the stage and continued with rehearsals.

During the break, while the dancers were changing into their new costumes, I went upstairs to the prop cupboard and found it empty. I closed the door, turned off the overhead light and sat in front of one of the computers. I went online to search for new talent, the images on the screen keeping others at bay. Hands like white boxing gloves. Alone in her room on Mother's Day.

The door opened and Gabriel Grosse came in.

He walked over to the sofa and tossed a cushion to the floor before he noticed me.

'Jesus fucking Christ, I didn't see you there.' He swept a stack of papers from the desk. 'Did I leave my phone here?' He looked at me. 'Sitting in the dark?'

'Someone died,' I said.

He looked confused. 'Who did?'

'My grandmother.'

'Your grandmother died . . . today?' His expression changed. 'Damn. I'm sorry, kid.'

'Thank you.' I turned my face away.

There was an embarrassed pause. 'If you, uh, wanna go home tonight . . .'

I shook my head. 'I'll be fine.'

'Good. That woman. Fucking cunt.'

I laughed. A bitter sound. 'Yes. Yes, she is.'

He was there in the room for the final dress rehearsal. 'Pretend I'm not here,' he told those present, as if that were in any way possible.

The dancers began the routine, a rehash of an old number. It ended clumsily as they stripped from the unfamiliar costumes that had been finished that day.

'What the fuck?' Gabriel Grosse turned to me as the music came to a stop.

The dancers and everyone in the auditorium fell silent.

'What the fuck are they wearing?'

'It's for the theme . . .'

'*It's for the theme*,' he mocked. 'Are you stupid?'

The room seemed to be receding.

'I . . .'

'Just stop fucking talking and fix it.'

'Whatever you want,' I heard a small voice reply.

'What are you, my *wife*?'

I looked beyond him to the door. *Leave*, I told myself.

But I stayed instead, and I fixed it.

After rehearsals, I went up to the VIP bar. Whisky poured halfway up the glass. An hour later, at ten o'clock, Mary Lamb's guests began to arrive.

In they came, the Chosen Ones, familiar faces from the pages of magazines, who in the flesh gave the unnerving impression of being lookalikes of themselves. Only the supermodel who moved with an insect-like grace, made heads turn when she entered, gurning only slightly, her delicate jaw rotating like mandibles.

Mary Lamb was patrolling the crowd, a murderous look on her face. 'Who are you?' She swooped on a pair of hostesses. 'I don't know you.'

'We work here.'

She glared at them, then moved away to continue her hunt for potential gatecrashers.

I stood by a pillar, watching them all. Behind my eyes, my thoughts shrieked and babbled, and I could not understand them.

The party creaked into life. On stage, someone was making a speech punctuated by lacklustre cheers from the crowd. A commotion at the back of the room announced the arrival of Rose, who appeared dressed as a homeless person wheeling a shopping trolley, from which dangled many small baggies heavy with what looked like faeces. As she reached the stage, Rose began pelting them at the crowd who ran for cover, squealing.

'Poetry.' Gabriel Grosse's voice at my shoulder.

I turned to see him smirking. His suit was so beautiful, and I understood that if I did not leave – right now – I would lose my mind entirely.

'Someone's looking for you,' a hostess called from the golden gun as I blundered through the lobby.

There was a flash of cameras outside. 'Ruby!' a voice cried from the queue as I ran from the alley without looking back.

A wall of sound hit me when I reached Old Compton Street, shoulders colliding with my own as I searched for a door – any door – that would take me somewhere outside myself. I swerved to the side to avoid a group of drunks. *I'm invisible*. That thought again. Resisting the urge to check my hands for transparency, I paused outside the window of a restaurant designed to resemble a run-down fish and chip shop, but everything was shiny, brand new. What had been there before? It seemed urgent I remembered. Inside, two diners looked at me curiously as I stumbled on.

At the French House the barman was yelling last orders. Despite the harsh yellow light, you could almost be in the

Soho of yesteryear. I fought my way to the bar through the booze-smelling crowd and threw my money down.

'We're all artists here,' a woman with red wine staining her lips was bawling in my ear. I identified her as one of the ageing soaks, a refugee from the old bohemia, my pity turning to revulsion at the idea she might consider us the same.

'No one's an artist anymore,' I told her. For a moment she looked injured, then her expression became haughty, and she drifted away.

Outside the temperature had dropped, a bitter wind blowing me in the direction of Dean Street. A pair of paparazzi was hovering outside the Groucho, waiting for someone to disgrace themselves. I'd been carried out of there once over somebody's shoulder, still wearing my showgirl costume. The image seemed to drift towards me and through. It shimmered on the corner, an interference in the night's fabric, wavering for a moment at the entrance to an alley. I followed, past the door with *This is Not a Brothel. There Are No Prostitutes at This Address* above the knocker.

Deranged neon and shrieking electronics from the late-night arcade, and I was back on Wardour Street headed for the Club. I turned the other way. Up ahead, a flicker. I moved towards it, a taxi blocking my path, and when it was gone only a dim-lit stairwell remained. I stepped through, towards the sounds and warmth emanating from below. Downstairs, the club was cave-like and smoky. A handful of people, no one in the cloakroom. In front of me, the bar appeared to glow. The wine would be cheap and sour, but I wouldn't care. I'd buy another, then another until the edges blurred and everything spoken is a delight.

*   *   *

'Someone's looking for you,' the hostess cried, swinging her legs in my direction.

Around her the lobby rotated slowly around the golden gun. I was back at the Club. Steadying myself against the sight, I held onto the banister to haul myself back up the stairs that bucked and swayed beneath me.

Inside, a shaggy-looking DJ was playing disco hits, Mary Lamb gyrating onstage like an angry go-go dancer. I blundered towards the side of the stage and made for the backstage corridor, which rocked like a boat in a storm.

'I can't believe people still go here,' a man was complaining in a Brooklyn whine. We were on the four-poster bed with a random woman, doing coke off someone's key.

'What do you do?' he asked me for the third time.

'I direct the show.'

'Huh. I must be the first interesting person you've met for a long time.'

'What's your name?' I asked.

'I fucking told you already.'

Opposite, in a makeshift fortune teller's booth beneath a red neon sign, Russella was reading tarot for a drunken blonde woman.

Mary Lamb appeared in the doorway and glowered in their direction. 'Your last reading was shit.'

'Sorry,' said Russella.

'Do it again,' said Mary Lamb. 'This time do it properly.'

The blonde woman looked as if she might protest, then thought better of it. Mary Lamb sat down in front of Russella, who handed her the deck.

'You whores have done all my fucking coke,' said the man, scraping the baggie with the key.

'Do you want to get more?' The woman smiled.

'You know someone?' His eyes lit up hungrily. A man in the grip of a binge.

On the other side of the room, I heard Russella say, 'You're a very negative person. You see the worst in everything.'

Mary Lamb was leaning forward, her eyes wide. 'Shit, you are good.'

The woman disappeared with the man's money, leaving us alone on the bed. He was talking about the film he was producing, the actors all morons and ingrates.

'You work here?' He was eyeing me in a different way.

I nodded, too high to speak.

'Christ, you must be bored.'

Bored? I turned the word over in my mind. I was beyond bored. So much so, it was possible I was having the time of my life. This is what we did. We partied. We were the Chosen Ones. This party, this bed, the beating heart of the best club in the world.

The woman returned with the Movie Star in tow. There was another party to go to, taxis being called.

'I'm with you,' the producer said to me.

I didn't respond, deep in the white and glittering place where speech no longer mattered.

*   *   *

The Movie Star was on the sofa, the magnetic field of his fame sucking the eyes of everyone in the room. They seemed to slant towards him, their mouths talking, talking, sentences that began with *I, I, I.*

The producer was pitching a film, his hand grasping the Movie Star's knee as if by claiming this territory he could claim his ear. The woman was leaning across the producer, pushing her beauty forwards, teeth first. Her hand touched another part of the Movie Star. His arm. On the other side of the room, the charmless man, our host, was drinking in the scene, taking surreptitious pictures on his phone.

I reached for the rolled-up note to bolster the chemical barrier against the encroaching day, my sudden awareness of crusted mouths and nostrils. I hadn't spoken since the Club.

Leaving them arguing over ordering more coke, I found my way to the bathroom. I sat on the toilet, my heart rabbit-fast, and squeezed out a few dehydrated drops.

There was a knock on the door. I opened it and the producer pushed his way inside, his mouth over mine. My dress around my waist, a shock of dryness and bristles, his face between my legs. And then he was standing, whispering urgent questions. I looked at him, mute, trying to understand what could have happened to him.

Alone again in the bathroom, I held onto the sink. In the mirror something in my eyes was screaming to be acknowledged. I went out to the hall and towards the front door.

'You can't fucking go. I told you, I'm with you.'

The producer followed me into the brutal March morning where a taxi waited in the cold light.

It was snowing when we reached the boat, sparse, bitter gusts that stung my face, the day every shade of white and grey.

'*I live on a boat*,' he mocked as we crossed the pontoons.

Inside, it was silent and freezing.

Downstairs, Felicity would be sitting in the kitchen, drinking tea. She'd know how to make him leave. Then I remembered, she lived in Brighton now.

'It's cold,' I said.

'This life is fast and hard, but it'll do for now.'

Did you rehearse that? I tried to say, but no sound came out.

In my cabin, he stripped the dress from my body, my tights getting stuck on my shoes.

Naked he was pitiful, soft and potbellied.

We fell to the bed, and I knew with a flash of clarity, to have sex with this man would be a soul death from which I might never recover.

'You're not gonna fuck me?' he said, understanding.

'No.'

There was fractured dialogue amidst grappling, his hand dragging on my hair.

'You're not gonna suck this big cock?'

'It's not that big.'

We were on the edge of the unthinkable. I did the only thing I could think of to prevent either of us making a choice. He came almost instantly and rolled to the side, gasping.

'Fuck,' he said. 'That was hot.'

I sat up. My hand wet with him.

'Please go,' I said.

'Fuck you. I'm not going anywhere.'

I started to cry.

'Oh god, you're freaking out. Why are you freaking out?'

I closed my eyes.

'I lost someone today. I shouldn't have been partying.'

'Oh shit,' he said. 'Hey, c'mere.' The producer pulled me down. 'We all need a little love sometimes,' he said and drew my arms around him.

'*Get the fuck off my boat! Get the fuck off my boat!*'
   In the mirror, the naked screaming girl looked wild.
Finally, I recognised her.

Chapter 20

When the producer had gone, I took two Valium and crawled beneath the covers, curling into myself until I felt it dull the edges of my broken-glass thoughts, reaching for its touch like a lover.

Sometime later, my heart shocked me awake. I lay still for a long time, focusing on its beat. It was dark in my cabin, cold and quiet. I got up and dragged the sheets from my bed and carried them to the washing machine. Then I took a bath.

I stayed in the water until it turned cold, then went upstairs and sat in front of the heater in my towel, the heat from its orange bars burning my face. Outside, snow was still falling, dissolving into puddles on deck. Silence from the road. Not another soul in London.

If this is the bottom, I thought, you must start again and find out what you lacked.

I reached beneath the chaise and pulled my laptop from its hiding place and began a new email: *Dear Gabriel.*

I would do it face-to-face. I would do it calmly with the minimum of fuss. I would explain why.

My hands shook a little as I dressed myself the following day. Gabriel Grosse had replied, agreeing to a meeting. *Midday.*

I looked at my clothes hanging on the rail, the glossy wardrobe his money had paid for. I found an old pair of jeans and put them on and made my face up carefully.

The snow had disappeared during the night, crisp spring sunshine giving the streets a freshly washed feel. I took the shortcut through the World's End to wait for the bus to Soho.

At the Club, I took three flights of stairs directly to the boardroom. Knocking once, I stepped inside.

The OM was sitting at the far end of the long table. He gestured to the chair nearest the door.

'Where's Gabriel?' I asked.

'Gabriel's not coming today.'

I laughed then, understanding that – of course – I was being fired.

He began to speak, and I raised my hand. 'Shall we save ourselves some time?'

By the time I reached my bus stop an email had been sent, cc-all, announcing my departure and wishing me the best for the future. I turned my phone off as the first bewildered messages from the performers began to arrive.

Fuck Gabriel Grosse. This was the phrase that kept me going in the days that followed, insulating me from pain, along with a dizzying sense of relief. I was free.

I moved around the boat like someone waking from a dream, hours on the chaise staring into space, hands cradling a cold mug of tea. With nothing to do and nowhere I had to be, grief crept in slowly and I welcomed its arrival. A heaviness of body; even the air had more weight.

The funeral would be held in a fortnight's time. When I spoke to my parents, I found I had strong opinions about the arrangements. No, the village hall near the church would not do; rejecting the photograph they'd chosen for the order of service for one of my grandmother, whisky in hand, laughing at a dinner a few years back. I heard myself tell my father that I would write the eulogy.

But how to tell the story of anyone's life, let alone someone you love?

A week went by. I went to bed before midnight, waking with the sun to watch the river slowly come to life. I took long walks in the park and thought about my grandmother.

One day I began to write, *GJ had a lot of secrets . . .*

Two hours later, I looked up from my laptop, dazed, as I came back to my body. It was done.

The morning of her funeral, I put on a dark blue dress I'd worn at the Club in a different way, my nerves worse than any I'd experienced before stepping on stage. I'd done so much in front of audiences, but never spoken as myself. I did not trust that the words would come, imagining the humiliation of a quavering voice, or no voice at all.

Outside the doors of the pretty church my grandmother had selected herself, a man in motorcycle leathers was hovering, clutching an enormous bunch of white roses. My old boyfriend, the one who'd adored her.

When it was my turn to read, I propped my papers on the lectern, hands either side to stop them from shaking. But when I opened my mouth, fear fell away.

And as I tried to give her back all that she'd lost, I could feel her there inside the story; and when I saw people smile and heard their gentle laughter, I knew that here could be alchemy of a different kind.

٭ ٭ ٭

Aftermath. There is drama in a funeral – a kind of show, after all – but when it was over and the white rose I'd kept from my old boyfriend's bouquet had wilted on the kitchen counter, I was left on the boat with my thoughts.

Spurred on by change, I went to bed early, to the swimming pool and the supermarket, filling the fridge with green vegetables and fruit. But it didn't take long before the reality of my situation dawned. I had another month's wages in the bank but after that there was nothing. I hadn't saved a penny. Pride would not allow me to ring around my old cabaret contacts, so I went online to investigate how others sought gainful employment, lost in impossible fantasies of starting again in faraway countries. But such a leap of faith would require both resources and energy that I no longer possessed.

Rose emailed me from Mexico where she was recovering from surgery. She did not mention the Club, or the fact I was no longer there. Having no news of my own, I wrote back that I missed her, because it was true. No one else tried to contact me, I wondered how long I'd taken to erase, a month? A week maybe. For a while I was angry and then grew sad again because I could not hate Gabriel Grosse. He'd set out to create a marvellous game to make the people come, and he'd achieved it. But the Club was as broken as him; a loveless place. No one could find satisfaction there, with all the money in the world.

April became May and May became June. London not a place to be idle. Stranded on board with no purpose and no plan, I could feel the city leaving me behind. With the crew gone, the boat seemed unwholesome, run down and melancholic, somewhere only the lost would find refuge. Ashamed of my washed-up state, going out had little appeal. My phone still rang after midnight from time to time, calls from unfamiliar numbers with always the same demand: *Let me in.*

The weather grew warmer, and I spent hours walking up and down the King's Road, sometimes sitting on a bench to watch Chelsea go by. When watching got boring, I'd close my eyes and listen to fleeting scraps of conversation. One day, I heard someone muttering beside me. 'You fucking bastards,' the Bird Lady was saying. 'You pissing fucking cunts.'

On a hot night in early July, I was heading home with a bottle of wine when I passed a man busking outside the station, who I recognised from after-hours Soho. He asked me where was I going, and could he come? And because I had nothing to do the following day, or any day after that, I said yes. He was already drunk, bare-chested beneath his waistcoat. He stayed for a week, and I welcomed the company. We'd start drinking by lunchtime, falling asleep at odd hours. It was high summer in London, the air on the Embankment thick with heat and petrol fumes. To cool off, we'd run through the fountains in Battersea Park, and at night he'd play the boat's collection of broken guitars, and I could almost convince myself we were a couple of rolling stones, laughing in the face of life. Though in truth we were both too old to be so carefree.

One day, he took me to the home of a society drug dealer, the walls decorated with originals by Banksy. On the way to the toilet, I heard noises coming from the bedroom and two teenage girls appeared – fresh out of boarding school – one of them bearing the marks of self-harm on her slender arms. The dealer put the kettle on for tea and laid out a plate of cocaine laced with MDMA and ketamine, which the girls fell on greedily. I took a biscuit instead, afraid of finding myself there the next day.

The guitarist lived above a bookshop in Fitzrovia where we'd return from boozing our way around the same small streets. One night, rotted from drink, we went back to the flat and the guitarist put his own album on the record player. We sat listening to his guttersnipe blues mourning Soho's halcyon days with well-worn cliché. *How many requiems does this town need?* I wondered. I may have said it out loud. The next day, I was woken by the sound of building works outside and left him sleeping there.

Freefall. Like wheeling through darkness unable to grasp anything to halt your descent. I'd wake heart pounding, my adrenalin in overdrive, stumbling through the day disorientated and frantic, seeking distraction of any kind, objects slipping from my newly clumsy hands. I was aware of reaching a point from which I was no longer certain of return. I'd known this nameless and physical terror, known it in many forms, escaping in the past by running headlong into sensation, my stories the trophies for having lived to tell the tale. But the Club had wrecked me, and I no longer knew how to find what happened next. And soon the boat would be gone.

It was August when Kristian knocked gently on my cabin door, where I was sleeping away the afternoon.

'The trapdoor was open,' he said.

I sat up and peered at him through my hair, the sunlight refracting from my mirror ball crash helmet casting a rainbow across one of his eyes.

'Why aren't you on tour?' I asked him.

'I had some time off.'

'And you came back *here*?' I shuffled out of bed. 'Weirdo.' I gave him a kiss and moved towards the corridor.

'Of course, you have to stay,' I said over my shoulder. 'But I'm afraid we're not around for much longer.'

'Have you packed?' Kristian followed me into the kitchen.

'What do you think?'

'I thought you might need a hand.'

Kristian went out the next day and returned with a stack of brown cardboard boxes, tape, and a large roll of bubble wrap, and together we began the gargantuan task of packing up the boat. Room by room, we labelled seven years' worth of accumulated paraphernalia as either 'trash' or 'treasure'. Most of it, we soon realised, was trash; an ancient set of the *Encyclopaedia Britannica* disintegrating when we moved it. What treasure we found, Kristian cleaned and wrapped to be taken to my parents' house to stow away in the attic. At least a dozen boxes were taken to the charity shops, along with half my clothes and books that had survived the damp.

The more we got rid of the lighter I felt. 'Let's just get rid of it all,' I said.

I left certain special items in random places, on benches, parks and garden walls for people to find. My feather fans and costumes I gave to performer friends, and I sold the egg to a burlesque dancer who'd make better use of it than I ever had. I told her to collect it from the Club and to ask for Archie. Soon there was little that remained but the chaise longue and my broken-down bed.

Without the junk, the boat's state of decay was more apparent than ever – some of the objects had been there so long they left a halo of grime on the wall – so I went to the hardware shop for cleaning supplies. We sponged down the walls, attacking the tobacco stains and cooking grease on the kitchen ceiling with sugar soap, scrubbing the oven for the first time in years. I used two packets of dusters, wiping the thick grey dust and mould from every shelf, porthole and corner, the boat emerging from beneath the dirt. It would be a military send-off.

To my surprise, it was the Cat who came to drive us to the dump on Kristian's last day. He'd had his hair cut short with a Caesar fringe that rather suited him. Despite the heat, he was wearing a girl's yellow raincoat done up with toggles.

'Hello, Dean,' I said.

'Miaow,' said the Cat.

In the kitchen, I made rounds of bacon sandwiches before we loaded the mountain of unsalvageable junk that was piled on deck into the Cat's van, which was parked in the loading bay being perused by an enthusiastic traffic warden.

At the Battersea dump, we had a fine time hurling everything in, smashing the broken guitars on the ground. Driving back to Chelsea, I was filled with love for the great-hearted boys on either side of me. Perhaps, I thought, to allow yourself to drift takes a different kind of bravery.

We said goodbye that evening, the Cat offering to drive Kristian to the station from where he'd be leaving for the next leg of his tour. When they'd gone, I sat by myself in the kitchen and opened a bottle of wine.

On the back wall above the wood burner, two puppets swung like garrotted children with the boat's gentle rocking. The last of my props. I walked over and lifted them down. Two little showgirls with wings, one of them dressed in feathers, the other sooty and singed.

Taking them in my arms, I carried them down the gangplank.

By night, the bridge crouched low and dark, lit by soft sulphur-coloured lamps. Standing at its middle looking down at the black water, I thought of the time I'd seen a man clinging to its railings, threatening to jump. He'd held on so long the river police had arrived, waiting nearby in their outboard motor. It was not a high bridge and they'd have fished him out immediately. It was hard to take him seriously. On either side of the bridge, a queue of red London buses waited in line.

The puppets were made from papier mâché and barely made a splash when they hit the water. They floated towards Putney, limbs dancing in the swirling current.

Curtain

The night before the pirates came, I lay awake listening to the sound of the Thames, watching the square of darkness above me for signs of the coming day. At four in the morning, it began to rain heavily, and I slipped naked out of bed and went out to the deck.

I stood looking over the water I knew so well. Years before, a bottle-nosed whale had lost its way and swum up the river, beaching itself in the shallows opposite. I'd watched in amazement as the crowd looking on from the bank moved as one, men tearing off their ties, rushing down to the water to push the whale back to the safety of the depths. It had died in the end; its bones now lay in the Natural History Museum. But it had shown me a glimpse of something I hadn't known was there.

The city was full of stories such as this; the glorious, grand and awful. I'd always lived for mine – I was the girl things *happened to*. But who were those stories for, and who decided they were worth living? It all got swept out to sea, eventually.

What would it mean, to be the only one looking on?

I stood in the late summer storm until I started shivering and went back to bed.

Just before dawn, I heard the growl of the tug's engine. Pulling on some clothes, I went outside to meet them.

'I'll be coming with her,' I called down to the captain.

'Up to you, love,' he said. 'We won't be stopping though.'

The boat was untied, heavy coils of rope slapping wetly onto the pontoon, and I went downstairs to use the toilet before the waste was disconnected.

The hull vibrated as the tug's engine began to judder, and I fetched the bottle of champagne I'd been keeping in the fridge.

I climbed with it onto the roof, as the boat eased from her berth for the last time. There was a gleam of gold as we curved out in a wide arc, the Queen's barge *Gloriana* appearing from the west, her oars bright in the morning sun. Following in the barge's wake, we set off towards the City.

As we passed beneath the bridge, I thought I saw the Bird Lady waving from the shore.

Past the leafy banks of Battersea Park, the bright spire of the Buddha's pagoda rises between the trees as the boat moves towards the candy-coloured struts of Albert Bridge. In the distance the power station looms, towers bristling with cranes.

On towards Vauxhall, buildings become Oz-like with green glass, bridges groaning with traffic and noise. A police boat approaches at Westminster, then, realising any military threat the boat once possessed is long gone, returns in the direction it came, helicopters cruising in noisy circles overhead.

Onwards, past the gothic postcard of Parliament and Big Ben, the baleful stare of the London Eye. The river wider at Waterloo, an impossible cityscape climbing towards the sky.

Blackfriars and St Paul's, the twisted spine of the Millennium Bridge where people whoop and wave. The river now half a mile wide, the boat a wooden toy on its broad brown back. The Globe Theatre a gorgeous anachronism on the southern bank.

A train runs overhead at Cannon Street, and you travel under London Bridge without incident. On the HMS *Belfast* a wedding is taking place, and you send her a wish for a better end.

Tower Bridge – the last – lies ahead. She raises her sky-blue gates as the tug, tiny against her great flanks, charges her engines and you are out into the wide, wide river and the red bricks of Bermondsey.

The bottle is empty now, and you're weeping as if you'll never see the city again.

The Docklands, Wapping, Shadwell, Limehouse, Canary Wharf, Deptford, Greenwich. The *Cutty Sark* so long at anchor she's forgotten she's a boat.

Beyond the folly of the O2, something silvery and strange.

A row of squat, shining towers traversing the river from side to side. The Thames Barrier, beautiful and alien, gleaming in the sun.

Now the river is a sea, the boat no more than a husk, a torn page riding the swell.

On the roof you stand, as you pass on through.

Acknowledgements

Thank you to:

My wonderful parents for their unwavering support, and being very good sports.

My sisters, my first and forever coven, the funniest witches I know.

Emmanuel, Eva-Jane and Vivienne, keepers of my heart. Don't read this until you turn twenty-one.

Auntie C, for your love and infinite kindness.

GJ. You are with me, always.

My darling friends, my inner onion. For keeping my show on the road . . . thank you, thank you, thank you.

My godmother, Annie Turvey, who shared her love of the stage.

My first English teacher, Luna Rupchand, who shared her love of words.

MTB boat crew, Kristian, Bitz, Au Mat, the Cat . . . and all the crew who came before, whose influence and antics have made their way into this story.

The late Captain Alasdair Campbell, who entrusted the boat to me, with all the happiness that came after.

M., the brightest of us all, who first invited me to dance. How I wish you were still here.

The MA Creative Writing faculty at Birkbeck, especially Julia Bell and Russell Celyn-Jones without whom this book would not exist. Thanks also to the inimitable Jonathan Kemp and Toby Litt.

My Birkbeck #supergroup for the early reads and encouragement. See you at The Harrison?

My #breakawaygroup sisters, Lou Kramskoy, Louise Hare, and our beloved Karen Clark, so deeply missed.

Lesley Thorne, for her invaluable support and championing the book when it was still a half-made thing.

Sam Champtaloup and Alan Poul at Boku Films, for their vision, enthusiasm, and being generally very lovely.

The Society of Authors, for the helping hand.

Nettie Battam (Her Royal Knickers), who read the very first chapters, who cheered me on, and is a very naughty lady indeed.

Sophie Dean, Sarah Fielding, Kate Friend, Bobbie Greenish, Laura Pannack, Kirsten Pennefather (KG), Demelza Woodbridge and Brita Young, for their always wise words and talking me down from various ledges during the process of bringing this book to light. I'm so lucky to have you.

The Murray Mcanyana family, Nyasha, Sabelo, Tanaka, Thandi and Lili. For making our house such a happy home.

Héloïse Werner (little one!), who listened to 'bed stories' in the blue city of Chefchouen, who introduced me to . . .

. . . my wonderful, hilarious agent John Ash, who balances brilliance with genuine care. Thank you for everything.

. . . and also, magician Raphaël Neal, who took my extremely flattering headshot, and has captured many moments in my life so beautifully. There's no one I'd rather get naked in the bluebells with.

The incredible team at Coronet/Hodder. My whip-smart, passionate and very glamorous editor, Harriet Poland. I'm so glad it was you. And the brilliant Tom Atkins, who took over editorial duties, thank you for adopting me and taking such good care of my book. Publicity genius Maria Garbutt-Lucero, dream publisher Hannah Black, and Will Speed for the perfect cover design.

To Rose, if this book has a muse, it's always been you. Thank you for our conversations – long may they continue – and for sharing your extraordinary, beautiful mind with me.

A very special thank you to all the performers for their generosity in allowing me to tell a tiny fragment of their story. You are my inspiration. My greatest hope is that I've done you justice.